Dialogue with Life

Dialogue with Life

MADHU DANDAVATE

ALLIED PUBLISHERS PRIVATE LIMITED
NEW DELHI MUMBAI KOLKATA CHENNAI NAGPUR
AHMEDABAD BANGALORE HYDERABAD LUCKNOW

ALLIED PUBLISHERS PRIVATE LIMITED

Regd. Off. : 15 J.N. Heredia Marg, Ballard Estate, Mumbai 400001
12 Prem Nagar, Ashok Marg, Opp. Indira Bhawan, Lucknow 226001
Prarthna Flats (2nd Floor), Navrangpura, Ahmedabad 380009
3-2-844/6 & 7 Kachiguda Station Road, Hyderabad 500027
5th Main Road, Gandhinagar, Bangalore 560009
1/13-14 Asaf Ali Road, New Delhi 110002
17 Chittaranjan Avenue, Kolkata 700072
81 Hill Road, Ramnagar, Nagpur 440010
751 Anna Salai, Chennai 600002

First Published 2005
© Author
ISBN 81-7764-856-X

ISBN 13: 978-81-7764-856-0

In memory of

Prem Bhasin

A valiant freedom fighter and a dedicated socialist,

my source of strength and inspiration

ACKNOWLEDGEMENT

Dr. Usha Prasad of the Oral History Division of the Nehru Museum and Library interviewed me extensively. Her quest began with the early influences on my life, and then she proceeded to trace its further evolution through various phases against the background of educational, cultural, social, economic and political environment. These interviews form the basis of this book, *Dialogue with Life*.

Uday and Rohini Dandavate undertook the painstaking work of editing the manuscript.

The beautiful cover illustration by Shekhar Godbole, the author's photograph by Shailan Parker and the attractive cover design by Uday Dandavate contribute an aesthetic touch to this publication.

I am grateful to Allied Publishers for their elegant production.

I express my deep gratitude to all of them.

Madhu Dandavate

PREFACE

The Oral History Division of the Nehru Memorial Museum and Library approached me for a comprehensive interview about my life, endeavours, struggles, commitments and political and ideological orientations.

I feel interviews are a more effective medium of communication than one's memoirs, which tend to become a monologue, with the reader becoming just a passive entity at the receiving end. On the other hand, during an interview based on sharp and searching questions by the interviewer, one has to be more transparent and communicative. He has to reveal more than what he would have in his self-portrayed memoirs. Thus such interviews, in effect, become a vocal *'Dialogue with Life'*.

With hindsight, as I cast a glance at the evolution of my life from its formative stages to the present turbulent times, I realize that there is an imperative need to inculcate in our personal and social life, human values like freedom, equality, social justice, religious tolerance, secularism, environment friendliness, dignity and empowerment of women, and above all a scientific temper for ensuring social and economic reconstruction. However, the scientific temper has to be harnessed not merely for the creamy layers of society. It has to be harmonized with the needs of the poor and the deprived who dwell in 7,00,000 villages of India, many of them living below the poverty line. If they are made to suffer in silence for long, that silence may one day explode with all its fury and destroy the gains of the technological revolution sweeping across our country today. Gandhiji gave this warning to the nation in his lifetime, a warning that we can overlook only at our own peril.

In the pre-Emergency period, the movement in Bihar and Gujarat against corruption, subversion of democracy and failure to expedite electoral reforms led to the rise of dynamic youth power. Jayaprakash Narayan saw the great potentiality of an instrument of change in this.

The 1984 anti-Sikh riots, the demolition of the Babri Masjid and arson, murders and looting in Gujarat during the recent communal holocaust struck a heavy blow to secularism. The spirit of religious tolerance, which was nurtured with great care during India's freedom struggle, lay in shambles. However from the ashes of these shambles will one day rise the edifice of harmonious India. Passion is momentary but compassion is more enduring.

All my life I have fought against injustice, and participated in constructive activities to build a new society. I have tried to give voice to the agonies and aspirations of the poor and the neglected through vigilant activism on the forum of Parliament as well as struggles outside. This has been my humble contribution to fulfill our cherished dreams. The future may be dim, but not totally dark. As the famous poet, the late Kaifi Azmi had rightly said:

> *A wave of anger*
>
> *Blew away the lamps*
>
> *But, yes, one remained;*
>
> *Its name is hope, and it flickers on*

New Delhi
1 July, 2005   **Madhu Dandavate**

CONTENTS

1

Early Influences

Politico-Cultural Background

I was born in Ahmednagar, on 21 January 1924.

Ahmednagar is a historically important place in the state of Maharashtra. It was in Ahmednagar where Chand Bibi, the Muslim princess, fought against the Mughals, displaying her bravery and valour. Later it became a place of pilgrimage for the freedom fighters because during the Quit India movement in 1942, the Ahmednagar Fort became a prison for Jawaharlal Nehru, Maulana Abul Kalam Azad, Acharya Narendra Deva, Sardar Vallabhbhai Patel and several other members of the Congress Working Committee. Some leaders wrote valuable books while in detention in Ahmednagar. Jawaharlal Nehru wrote his famous work, *The Discovery of India*, and Maulana Azad wrote the book *Ghubar-e-Khatir,* which is a collection of his literary experiences. Acharya Narendra Deva also started writing *Baudha Dharma Darshan*. Ahmednagar was also well-known for eminent leaders who tried to give shape to the politics of the country, and of the State.

My early influences were from my grandfather's literary works, my father's literary background, my mother's interest in social work and my aunt's deep involvement in poetry. My grandfather was a man of literature. He translated the plays of Bhas, the famous Sanskrit poet and the valuable work, Kautilya's *Arthashastra.* This translation was later included in the curriculum of the Pune University. He had also translated a number of poems written by Rabindranath Tagore. These translations were lost and hence remained unpublished. My father's sister, Manorama, was a poetess and was married to another literary figure, Sridhar Balkrishna Ranade, from Maharashtra. A member of Ravikiran Mandal, the pioneer organization of poets in Maharashtra, she wrote a number of poems in Marathi. Manorama and S.B. Ranade published a book titled *Sri-Manorama*. The literary influences of the members in my family were one of the factors that had a great impact on me.

We had a large collection of books by Gandhi, Swami Vivekananda, Gopal Krishna Gokhale and other eminent litterateurs and social reformers of Maharashtra. Our library at home also included works of Shakespeare and other renowned English authors, and the complete *Mahabharata*. With these resources being easily accessible, I developed keen interest in reading during the early years of my life. I think that this extensive reading nurtured in me the habit of writing articles on political and social issues at a later stage.

My reading included speeches and works of Lokmanya Tilak, Mahatma Gandhi, Jawaharlal Nehru, Gopal Krishna Gokhale, Sane Guruji, and several other patriots and social reformers. I studied works of social reformers like Mahatma Jyotiba Phule and Dr B.R.Ambedkar.

Later I had the opportunity to read literature on the life and thoughts of the Buddha. The study of the works and philosophies of these great thinkers lent a new balance to my social, economic and political thinking. The following quote by Kuan Chung, an educationist, had a deep impact on me. "If you plan for a year, plant a seed. If for ten years, plant a tree. If for a hundred years, teach the people. When you sow a seed once, you will reap a single harvest. When you teach the people, you will reap a hundred harvests".

Another couple that frequented our home in Ahmednagar was Malati, my father's sister, and her husband Madhavrao Pingle. Both had participated in the freedom struggle and had courted arrest. Madhavrao Pingle, popularly known as Pingle Guruji, had participated in various struggles in 1930, 1942, etc., and undergone rigorous imprisonments. He taught in a nationalist school at Bordi in Maharashtra with many other Gandhians. Achyut Patwardhan and P.H. Patwardhan (Raosaheb Patwardhan) were the other two people I knew, who participated in the Freedom struggle.

My close association with my aunt Malati and Madhavrao contributed to cultivating in me a sense of patriotism while influences of my grandfather, father, mother, a social worker, collectively developed in me an aptitude for literature.

Education

I went to a primary Municipal School in Ahmednagar. For secondary education I joined the Ahmednagar Education Society until my Matriculation examination. The late Justice M.G. Ranade, a great social reformer, scholar and a towering figure in the judiciary, founded this school. Eminent patriots and former members of the Congress Working Committee like Rao Saheb Patwardhan (P.H. Patwardhan), Achyut Patwardhan, revolutionary Senapati Bapat were in the same school. It was a premier educational institution at that time.

During my school years, I had varied interests. I had interest in poetry. Whenever there were poetry recitation competitions in the school, I would participate. Sometimes we had to recite from plays and that interested me too. I also developed a deep interest in the game of cricket and won many awards. My father encouraged me to play because he shared my love for cricket. My father felt that Bombay was a better place for developing and pursuing my interest in cricket and so, after graduating from school. I went to Bombay for my college education. I studied in Ramnarain Ruia College in the discipline of science for two years and later joined the Royal Institute of Science, one of the premier science institutions in Bombay. I got my Bachelor of Science and Master of Science degrees in Physics from this Institute.

My father was a civil engineer and wanted me to study engineering, but I preferred physics and aspired to be in the teaching profession in a University. So, much against the wishes of my father, I pursued Physics and later taught Physics in the Siddharth College of Arts and Science in Bombay and also at the Post-Graduate level in Bombay University. Late Dr B. R. Ambedkar, the Chairman of the People's Education Society, had founded the Siddharth College in 1945.

Roots of Social Justice

I remember a very strange and interesting experience in my early life. When I was in the primary class, we were given two booklets, one on the *Ramayana* and the other on the *Mahabharata*. A few days afterwards, my teacher in the primary school asked me, "Who do you feel was the hero of the epic Ramayana? I replied, "Sita was a greater personality than Rama". The teacher was visibly disturbed and his response was "The whole world accepts Rama as the great hero of the *Ramayana* and you say Sita was greater than Rama!" My young mind felt that only because she happened to be a woman and because some people expressed doubts about her character after her liberation from the captivity of Ravana, Rama asked her to face the ordeal by fire. In the epic it turned out that she succeeded and established her strength of character. However to my innocent mind subjecting her to such an ordeal was an act of injustice. I felt that Sita was nobler than Rama. About the *Mahabharata* my responses were similar. During my childhood I never knew what social justice was or its philosophy. It was beyond my comprehension as I was just a child. So I told my teacher that I was pained to find that when Ekalavya went to Dronacharya to learn the art of archery, he was denied that right on the basis of his caste, as he happened to be from the tribal community. Being determined to learn the art of archery he installed a statue of Dronacharya to seek inspiration. He worked hard to learn the art of archery and secure proficiency. Dronacharya was thrilled by his performance in the art of archery and said, "I had told you that you were not entitled to learn the art of archery, even then you have learned the skill". Ekalavya replied, "I will be happy to pay my dues for the alleged lapse." (I felt it was not a lapse.) Dronacharya's response was, "Cut off your thumb and give it to me". Ekalavya complied with his request. I felt that as far as knowledge is concerned, there should not be any discrimination. This was my response at that age. I now feel that my present commitment to the principle of social justice was embedded in my mind from a very early age.

I was greatly influenced by the freedom fighters in Maharashtra, namely Acharya Javdekar, S.M. Joshi, N.G. Goray, Rao Saheb Patwardhan,, Achyut Patwardhan, and Sane Guruji who were a tower strength to build Rashtra Seva Dal, a youth organization dedicated to Democratic Socialism and Secularism I was deeply impressed by the writings of Lokmanya Tilak, Mahatma Gandhi, Gopal Krishna Gokhale and social reformers like Agarkar and Justice Ranade. Though I had read the works of Marx and Gandhi, in retrospect I feel that I was rather late in studying the works of social reformers like Jyotiba Phule, Dr Ambedkar and humanists like Buddha. These social reformers had made a frontal assault on the iniquitous caste system in the Hindu society and the social injustice perpetrated by it against the oppressed sections in our society. This study, though undertaken rather late, lent a better balance to my thinking and made me conscious of the degree and dimensions of the social injustice in our society. It induced in me a deep urge to fight against social injustice.

Impact of Dr Ambedkar

I was a Professor of Physics in Siddharth College of Arts and Science in Bombay run by the People's Education Society. Its Chairman was Dr B.R. Ambedkar. I once approached Dr Ambedkar to share some of his experiences with me. He consented to my request. One of them was his experience at the lake in Mahad in the district of Kulaba in Maharasthra. The lake was called 'Chavdar Talav' (lake with tasty water) in Marathi. He decided to launch a satyagraha to secure freedom for the Dalits to drink water from that lake. He said, "I told my followers that the orthodox group will attack you but our weapon has to be compassion and not passion for violence". With a strong belief in in peaceful methods, they won the battle.

Dr Ambedkar's argument was that if high caste Hindus and animals could consume the water from the lake, Dalits should also have equal privilege because air and water belong to all.

Another interesting incident Dr Ambedkar narrated was about his resignation from the Union Cabinet on the question of the Hindu Code Bill. The essence of the Hindu Code Bill was to give women the right of inheritance to property and wealth. Not only was the orthodoxy against it but also some Dalit followers of Dr. Ambedkar wondered why he was forcing this issue. They were of the view that Dalits had nothing to gain or lose with the passage of this bill, since they did not have property and wealth and the question of inheritance for women would never arise in a Dalit family. Dr Ambedkar fervently pleaded for the bill because he felt that women were oppressed in our society, irrespective of their caste and community. Even the millionaires of high caste and high-class families ill-treated their widows. Women were secluded and forced to live a life of misery, hardships and sorrow on the loss of their husbands. He pointed out "This being the state of a widow in Indian society, I treat all women as a deprived section of the society and hence wish to stand up for their right of inheritance."

The experiences which Dr Ambedkar kindly shared with me had a deep impact on my mind.

I read Marx, starting with the *Communist Manifesto* of 1848, written in association with Engels. Then, I tried to study other classics of Marx including *Das Kapital*, which I found very difficult to grasp initially since I was not a student of Economics. Then I also read *Dialectical Materialism* by Plekhanov, *The Civil War in France* by Marx, and *State and Revolution* by Lenin.

In my youth, I was thrilled by Marxian classics. But later on, I realised that their rigid application without any thought for the objective conditions in society would destroy the very substance of Marxism.

Varied Interests

I developed an aptitude for literature, poetry, Indian classical music, Beethoven's symphonies and Mozart's music. Though I enjoyed listening to music I never became a singer or a musician. I enjoyed watching art films and theatrical plays on the stage in varied languages. I also developed great interest in fundamental sciences during my tenure as a teacher in Bombay University. I am proud that the famous Space Physicist, Kasturi Rangan, happens to be my former student.

My interest in cricket brought me some awards. I have fond memories of the cricket matches between the Lok Sabha and Rajya Sabha cricket teams. I had the honour of being the captain of the Lok Sabha cricket team. I received a silver shield as the skipper of the winning Lok Sabha cricket team from the President of India.

Imprisonments

I have been imprisoned several times by the government of free India, while offering satyagraha on people's burning problems and their grievances. During the solitary moments in the prisons in different parts of the country, I developed a habit of writing a pictorial diary that reflected my responses to various events. This activity provided a pleasant diversion from the routine political work. These imprisonments served as opportunities for reflection and writing.

To systematize and refine my views on political, social, economic and international issues, I have written several articles in English, Hindi and Marathi journals. Some of them have evoked animated debates both in the media and amongst people.

Underground Work

I participated in the Quit India movement of 1942 at the age of 18. Several political leaders influenced me in my childhood and youth. I was inspired to participate in the 1942 movement and I felt that merely offering satyagraha and going to jail was not enough. Mahatma Gandhi had said in 1942, that ". . . if I am arrested, everyone should consider himself to be his own leader and should be dictated by his own conscience". So, several leaders, particularly Socialist leaders, had undertaken the work of organising an underground movement. Being aware that I was young, not known as a public figure and with no chance of being identified by the police I could carry on with underground activities. The directorate of the underground movement had given instructions to destroy symbols of British imperialism, whether they were ammunition depots, railway centres, or court buildings, without destroying the lives of human beings. There was a Bench Magistrate's Court just on the border of Ahmednagar City in Maharashtra. So, in the darkness of the night, my young colleague Joshi and I collected some explosive material soaked in kerosene, broke the lock of the Bench Magistrate's Court, and set it on fire. My aunt and her husband, Pingle Guruji, were the only people who knew about this. The Court building was totally gutted. With the Court being in the outskirts of the city, it took a while before the police noticed the flames and the fire. My father was the Chief Officer and engineer in the Ahmednagar Municipality and the fire brigade was under its jurisdiction. He never knew at the time of the fire extinguishing operations that his son had set the court on fire.

My colleagues and I tried to disrupt sensitive telephone communications of the army headquarters. A couple of times I also tried to remove the fishplates of the railway tracks on which special military trains were expected to run, though not with much success. We also used to circulate underground literature. An English underground fortnightly journal, *Ninth August,* was edited by the underground leader Achyut Patwardhan and was meant for all-India circulation. There was another underground journal in Marathi titled *Krantikari.* Sane Guruji edited it. I clandestinely distributed these materials along with a group of college students. These activities gave us an opportunity to contribute in the underground movement and participate in the freedom struggle.

I was greatly inspired during the 1942 struggle by the work and writings of Mahatma Gandhi, Lokmanya Tilak, Subhas Chandra Bose, Yusuf Meherally and the underground leaders like JP, Achyut Patwardhan, Dr Rammanohar Lohia, Aruna Asaf Ali, Sane Guruji, S.M. Joshi, N.G. Goray and others. During the 1942 struggle my admiration for Mahatma Gandhi grew immensely.

2

1942: Quit India Movement

As a young college student I was present at the Gowalia Tank Maidan (August Kranti Maidan), in Bombay on the morning of August 9,1942 because it was announced that the national flag would be unfurled there. Gowalia Tank Maidan is of historic importance because the AICC (All-India Congress Committee) session was held here on August 7 and 8, 1942, when Mahatma Gandhi had given the clarion call for 'Quit India.

I was in the Royal Institute of Science. I heard the speech delivered by Mahatma Gandhi at the Congress session in 1942. I was in college when the call given to the people was 'Do or Die' and the warning given to the British was 'Quit India'.

Mahatma Gandhi wanted his message to be heard all over the world, so he delivered his speech both in Hindi and English. I was present as a visitor in that session and was deeply moved and inspired by its proceedings. I had seen Gandhi from a distance at prayer meetings. I was greatly influenced by Marxist literature, which I read during my college days and I was attracted towards Marxism, but after 1942, I realized that Mahatma Gandhi was the man who could move the entire nation.

Dream of Struggle

On the 1st August 1942, during Tilak's death anniversary meeting at the Chowpatty sands in Bombay, two speeches made a big impact on me. One was by Sardar Vallabhbhai Patel and the other one was by Yusuf Meherally, the Socialist leader, who was then the Mayor of Bombay. In his inimitable forceful style, Sardar Patel roared, "This will be the final struggle and it will not merely be a jail-going movement. We have to see that the government administration comes to a halt and ultimately the British quit India." It was a moving speech. Yusuf Meherally also spoke and exhorted that even if the leaders were arrested, youngsters must be prepared to carry on the final struggle with determination.

No party or group ever tried to take me in its own organization during my college days. During 1942, I became an ardent admirer of leaders like Jayaprakash Narayan. In 1942, the leadership of the Congress Socialist Party had suspended the party work, with instructions to all members of the party that everybody should collaborate with all the nationalist forces, which were in favour of the Quit India movement, and that in effect, they should not keep their separate identity as Congress Socialist Party members. Later a controversy arose about whether we should continue as the Ninth Augusters group or whether the Congress Socialist Party should be revived. Acharya Narendra Deva strongly felt that the Congress Socialist party should be revived. Following internal discussions the work of the Congress Socialist Party was revived.

For a while, I was in the student movement led by the Students Congress. Later on, in order to confront the Communists who were supporting the War, I had to be well versed in Marxism because they would try to browbeat us in the debates by profusely quoting from voluminous books on Marxism and take advantage of the ignorance of others. So, I read Marx elaborately as stated earlier. I will give you one instance. In our discussions, some Communists talked about the State. They asked me, "Do you understand the Marxian connotation of *State*?" I promptly replied, "Yes I do." I then quoted Lenin and his work *State and Revolution*. Lenin's connotation was, " State is a coercive instrument of class oppression based on violence and, therefore, you cannot just capture the capitalist state and use it for socialist transformation. It has to be destroyed by violence limb by limb". I convinced my Communist critics that they could not argue with me assuming that I was not well versed in Marxism. My study of Marxism also revealed to me various lacunae in Marxism.

Economics after Marx

During the underground movement, I came across a small pamphlet, written by Dr Ram Manohar Lohia. Its title was *Economics after Marx*. He had argued, "Rigid acceptance of Marxism or its rejection, both are wrong. Individuals can be there to guide you, but they cannot be the sole arbiters of your ideological commitments. You must examine every thinker's writings logically, on the touchstone of realities that existed". He also saw a lot of relevance in Gandhi's views.

So, during the 1942 movement, when there was disagreement with the Communists on issues of the War and Quit India movement, a separate organization, the Students Congress was formed. I took active part in it. Prior to the War, I was a sympathizer of that section of the Students Federation, which was led by the Communists, but later on I was very impressed by Jayaprakash Narayan. A young mind is often enamoured by the spirit of struggle. I admired his escape from the Hazaribagh Jail to carry on his underground work and his travels round the country to guide the underground movement in the Quit India struggle. He wrote three letters *To All Fighters of Freedom*. Few were aware that in the second letter Jayaprakash Narayan had stated that efforts were being made to establish contacts with Netaji Subhas Chandra Bose of the INA (Indian National Army) though there was no success in that direction. He stoutly defended Subhas Chandra Bose in his letter *To All Fighters of Freedom*. He had a literary style and an appeal for the youth. I still remember, the last paragraph of his first letter, "The sun of Indian freedom has already risen above the horizon. Let not the clouds of our own doubts and disputes, inaction and faithlessness obscure that sun and drown us in our self-created darkness". I was deeply influenced by those letters. Achyut Patwardhan and Aruna Asaf Ali contributed immensely in the underground movement. I had a great admiration for their work also.

RIN Revolt

These are some of the memorable events that steeled my will to freedom. In 1946 at Castle Barracks, in Bombay when the revolt by the naval ratings had taken place, the British Tommies, were walking around with their guns. In order to express our solidarity with the naval ratings in revolt, we had huge demonstrations in different parts of the city. I was on the Girgaum Road, when we heard that British soldiers with sten-guns would be coming to fire at the people demonstrating their solidarity with Royal Indian Navy (RIN) men in revolt. It was a narrow road and there was no way to escape. We tried to put stone barricades on the road to prevent the movement of military vehicles with British soldiers who went on firing at the demonstrators. They felt that demonstrators were creating barricades and before they built the barricades they wanted to frighten them away with indiscriminate firing. When we were at a small police station in Girgaum, the British soldiers came firing randomly at both the sides of the street. Many of us stood firmly with our backs against the wall and not worrying as to what would happen. I vividly remember how the person standing next to me was shot in the random array of bullets. While I was saved, many died during that firing. I almost felt that death and survival followed the law of probability. Life was very risky during the freedom struggle.

Here is another controversial incident in which I had played a considerable part. During the post-1942 struggle we had Students Congress conferences, and on the eve of one of the conferences, S.K. Patil, the leader of the Congress Party, had given the slogan, 'One Leader, One Party, One Programme'. The thrust of the slogan was to prevent ideological groups and parties like the Congress Socialist Party within the folds of the Congress. In the Students Congress conference I moved a resolution opposing S.K. Patil's move and my resolution was passed.

Congress Socialist Party

I have often been asked if I was ever a member of the Congress Socialist Party. Yes! Membership was restricted – on completion of six months of probation a full party membership card was given only if the work of the probationer was found satisfactory.

It was not as difficult to become a member of the Communist Party, but it was also not so easy. One filled the membership form and became a member and was put on probation for six months.

After working for six months as a probationer, the executive of the party branch would discuss the performance and activities of the probationer. In case of unsatisfactory work some probationers would be asked to continue their probation period for an additional six months. If their work was satisfactory, a full membership card was given. I got my full membership of the Congress Socialist Party in Bombay after six months of my probation.

A probationer was expected to work effectively in chosen areas such as youth and student front, women's organization, trade unions, tenants organizations, cooperative movement, party journals, kisan (farmers) front, conduct study classes, and work in elected civic bodies.

Yusuf Meherally was very keen about ideological training camps. Some literature had to be read by members. Yusuf Meherally had published a Socialist syllabus for study by members. Later on I wrote several articles for *Janata*, a Socialist weekly. At that time, Aruna Asaf Ali, Achyut Patwardhan and Jayaprakash Narayan were very active in developing *Janata* as an effective journal of the Socialist movement. Due to our active involvement in various activities, we were becoming quite strong, in Bombay, Bihar, U.P., Maharashtra, Orissa and Madhya Pradesh.

Underground Leaders

During the 1942 struggle, I was very much inspired by of the courage and convictions of certain underground leaders. JP was already arrested, and so was Dr Ram Manohar Lohia at a later stage. Till the British government withdrew the arrest warrants the police could not catch Achyut Patwardhan and Aruna Asaf Ali. In fact, there were many people whose contributions were not known to the people but were very significant to the 1942 struggle. For instance, Biju Patnaik, the leader from Orissa, took the underground leaders, Aruna Asaf Ali and JP in his small aeroplane to various places in India. In fact, Biju was a true daredevil. When Indonesians were being attacked, they requested Jawaharlal Nehru for help, since the Dutch army had surrounded their leaders. Biju Patnaik informed Jawaharlal Nehru that he could plunge into the encirclement by the army in his plane and liberate the trapped Indonesian leaders. It was interesting to hear about this incident from Biju in his own words when we were together in the Rohtak jail during the Emergency in 1975.

I feel proud of some of our old Socialist activists who participated with great courage in the 1942 movement. For instance, Yogendra Shukul, Suraj Narain Singh, Ramanand Mishra and others from Bihar, who escaped from Hazaribagh Jail along with Jayaprakash, showed exemplary bravery. While scaling down from jail walls, JP fell down and was hurt. Shukul and Suraj Narain put a hefty man like JP on their shoulders and carried him miles together. During the 1942 underground struggle, on one occasion, when Dr Ram Manohar Lohia and JP were arrested on the Nepal border and were kept in an impromptu jail guarded by policemen, members of the 'Azad Dasta' organization, which was an armed squad, attacked the jail and JP, Dr Lohia and others were liberated, though they were arrested again at a later stage. These stories of adventure of the underground activities of Jayaprakash, Dr. Lohia and others created a sense of thrill in the youth.

Underground Radio

I did not have initially any contact with the group that operated the underground radio. But later on after the arrest of Usha Mehta the prime mover of the underground radio, I developed contacts with Usha Mehta's colleagues who had helped her in the underground Radio project. Dr Ram Manohar Lohia had shared the idea of starting the underground Congress Radio with Usha Mehta. Being a very courageous lady, she took help from friends like Vithaldas Kanthabhai Jhaveri and Nanak Motwane to start the

Congress Radio. Nanak Motwane had come from Sind and was associated with Chicago Radio in Bombay. He had a lot of equipment. He gave the necessary equipment to Usha Mehta and she conducted the underground radio from various parts of Bombay city. She narrated to me at a later stage, after her release, how police came to raid their underground radio and arrested them. It was a novel idea! As soon as the police knocked at the door and asked her to stop the programme, she insisted on relaying the National Anthem 'Vande Mataram' on the underground radio. She told the Police Inspector, "Don't talk now; the National Anthem is going on". They stood in attention. On the completion of the anthem she said, "Now the National Anthem is over and our work is also over. You can arrest us." They were taken away. It was a great act of courage.

The intensity of the 1942 struggle continued for about a year, and it continued very well. Then the tempo of the struggle started waning. In my socialist activities, I was initially working mainly in Bombay. I was very proud that Asoka Mehta and JP had encouraged me in 1946 to take the responsibility of heading the Bombay Unit of the Congress Socialist Party as Secretary.

3

Birth of Socialist Movement

Nehru's relationship with the Socialists weakened gradually and on political issues the gulf between Jawaharlal Nehru and the Socialist leaders was widened. JP became the spokesman of the critical view against the Nehru government, especially in connection with the developments in the Soviet Union and East European countries like Hungary, Poland, Czechoslovakia, and also during the Chinese aggression. Jawaharlal Nehru's lukewarm attitude to these developments created a sense of disillusionment in the minds of Socialist leaders. The Socialists emerged as the most articulate critics of the Nehru government. The Socialists felt that Nehru, Tito and Nasser were the architects of the Non-alignment policy to which the Socialists were committed. This was being sabotaged. Acharya Narendra Deva had started realizing that in the field of planning and development too, Jawaharlal Nehru was relying on outdated structures.

Over the years, our attitude to Jawaharlal Nehru and response to his policies went through significant changes. In 1934, when the Congress Socialist Party was formed, many people believed that Jawaharlal Nehru had blessed this new formation. In the early days of the Socialist movement, the Congress Socialist Party had adopted a pro-Soviet approach. It was very appreciative of the Russian Revolution of 1917. The party supported the developmental model of Soviet Russia and considered Soviet Russia a friend of India. Closer to the declaration of 'Quit India' movement in 1942, the differences between Jawaharlal Nehru and the Socialists increased. All the way till the Quit India resolution was discussed in the Congress Working Committee, Jawaharlal Nehru maintained that India could not afford to launch a struggle for freedom in the midst of the War, as it would damage the cause of democracy. Inside the Congress Working Committee he had expressed this view very clearly. Socialists, along with men like Sardar Patel, Acharya Narendra Dev, Acharya Kriplani and others, maintained a firm position on the issue of launching a movement. Ultimately it was Mahatma Gandhi, who made a passionate plea to the members of the Congress Committee that the movement must be launched. Finally, Nehru relented and moved the resolution himself.

The Socialists had assured Mahatma Gandhi that they were firmly with him on his resolve to launch the 'Quit India' movement and would not let him down. The events preceding the launch of the Quit India movement in 1942 underscores the role Socialists played in forcing the decision through Congress Working Committee. At the AICC session, held on August 7-8, 1942 in Bombay at Gowalia Tank, Acharya Narendra Deva strongly pleaded for the Quit India Resolution. This episode reflects the weakening of the relationship between the Socialists and Nehru.

The Nasik session of the Socialist Party in 1948 was a momentous session. At the convention of the Party, Acharya Narendra Deva moved the political resolution. One paragraph was about our relations with the Congress. He said " Time has come when we have to part company with the Congress. The Congress was a multi-class organization in which all class organizations were united during our fight against the British. Now, after the attainment of freedom, parties based on distinct ideologies are needed. It cannot be a loose organization. Therefore, time has come when we must revive the Socialist Party as a separate instrument outside the Congress". JP, Dr Lohia and Acharya Narendra Deva, were initially of the opinion that since Mahatma Gandhi was assassinated, acute refugee problems were created following India's partition and there was instability; it was not the right moment to part with the Congress, but they felt that the party cadres should guide us.

JP and Dr. Lohia undertook a tour of the country. They were convinced that the party workers, by and large, after seeing the way they had been treated in various States, wanted a Socialist instrument to be set up separately as a Socialist Party. In the meantime the Congress Party had decided to amend its constitution prohibiting any ideological group or party within the Congress. Though Acharya Narendra Deva was a protagonist of the view favouring continuation of the party's association with the Congress in view of India's partition and the consequent instability in the country, he too changed his views when he found that the Congress high command wanted to prohibit any party within the Congress by amending its constitution suitably. Acharya Narendra Deva moved the political resolution at the session of the Socialist Party at Nasik in 1948, which was passed unanimously.

Ends and Means

JP as the General Secretary of the Socialist Party, presented his report. In the Report he rejected the notion 'ends justify the means' and emphasized that we must have fair means to achieve the fair ends. He cited Stalinist methodology which did not accept any scruples in achieving power, whether personal power or power for the party. In his report he expressed the view that if we accept the notion that ends justify the means, and set our eyes on power as the end goal, then there would be no limit on how far the means will sink to achieve those ends. Mahatma Gandhi emphasized the need for political workers to maintain the propriety of the means while pursuing political ends. JP suggested that Socialists would overlook Gandhi's prescription only at the cost of their own vision.

The consequence of the Nasik resolution of the Socialist Party had great moral overtones. When we decided to leave the Congress in 1948, there were 14 Socialist members in the U.P. Legislative Assembly. Obviously we had won on the Congress ticket. So immediately after our conference, Acharya Narendra Deva and his colleagues in the U.P. Legislative Assembly told the Speaker, "Sir, we were in the Congress. We have now left the Congress and have no moral right to continue in the Assembly". Govind Ballabh Pant, the Chief Minister responded "Acharyaji, *aap ke bina yeh mehfil chalegi nahi"*. Acharya Narendra Dev replied, "It will go on without us. That is the compulsion of political morality". The Speaker said, " There is no Anti-Defection Law!" Narendra Deva responded, " I am not guided by the written law; I am guided more by the inner moral law of life. All 14 of us are resigning". Out of 14, one seat was won uncontested. Otherwise all 13 candidates including Acharya Narendra Deva were defeated. But how did he take the defeat? Journalists asked him, "Acharyaji, what is your response to the defeat of all of you?" He replied, "It is only a warning to us that lot of work needs yet to be done. We did the right thing; it set the tone for future politics". When I think of that statement of Acharya Narendra Deva about the moral tone of politics and compare it with the present day politics, we find that today, politicians are selling their soul for patronage, wealth, and power. Even after the formulation of the Anti-Defection Law, which has been incorporated in Schedule X of the Indian Constitution, the situation has not changed. There is a loophole in the Anti-Defection Law at present, i.e. those who leave the party, will be disqualified as the members of the party on whose ticket they are elected. However, those who leave the party, with more than one-third of the membership of their party, will not attract the provisions of that Anti-Defection Law and they will continue as Legislators. This loophole is dangerous, in terms of criminal law, because it means that if an individual commits a criminal act he is a criminal, but if it is done collectively it is a pious act. In this context, the contrast between the moral postures that Acharya Narendra Deva took, and what we find today, becomes obvious. Governments have been formed and dissolved merely on the basis of numbers as a consequence of change of sides. Hardly any party has escaped from defections. So this is really the warning. At long last loopholes in Anti-Defection Law have been plugged.

Ideological Differences

It was not the clash of personalities that became the reason for Socialists to leave the Congress party, while the Congress government was in power.

Instead, it was the ideological differences that led to the Socialists leaving the Congress Party. The objective of the united national front of all classes and sections under the banner of the Congress to fight against imperialism was achieved, and there was no sense in remaining in the Congress without sharing ideological perspectives. It would have been a very loose structure in which nobody would have achieved anything. Our Socialist initiatives and identity would have been lost. I think the ideologically based division was inevitable. Prior to taking the decision to quit the Congress, in Bombay, our Socialist Party unit fought the Bombay Municipal Corporation (elections) as a separate entity against the Congress, and for the first time the Congress Party's absolute majority in the Corporation was lost, though the Congress emerged as the single largest party.

When Dr Lohia, Prem Bhasin and others launched satyagraha at the Nepalese Embassy in New Delhi in support of the democratic forces in Nepal, teargas was used against Dr Lohia and other satyagrahis. This led to a deep antagonism between Jawaharlal Nehru and Dr Lohia. This incident became a precursor to the widening gulf between the two leaders.

Relationship with Sardar Patel

JP has referred to an incident in one of his writings in the post 1942 period. During a casual encounter between JP and Sardar Vallabhbhai Patel, Patel put his hand on JP's shoulder and said, "I am highly appreciative of what you have done to support the 1942 struggle and the role you Socialists have played. Now the gap between you and me is reduced considerably. What would you like our government to do?" In response to his question, the Socialists put together a draft programme for the government's consideration. After reviewing the draft Patel responded, "This is a very bookish programme." Many years later, JP admitted, "To be very frank, today when I look back, I also feel that there was substance in Vallabhbhai Patel's comment." Many people thought that the Socialists were hostile to Sardar Patel and very supportive of Jawaharlal Nehru. This incident shows that there was indeed mutual admiration between Sardar Patel and the Socialists.

Congress Ban on Ideological Groups

The changed constitution of the Congress Party completely barred the forming of an ideological group. Acharya Narendra Deva on observing this change felt we were committed to ideas and values, which bound us by a social, economic and political perspective. If propagation of our Socialist ideology through an organized group were not permitted inside the Congress, we would have become merely an integral part of a heterogeneous flock. Therefore, the issue became debatable even for those who saw some substance in preserving past links with the Congress. It became necessary for us to sever the links with the Congress Party and become an independent group. What I would say is that in severing our links with the Congress and emerging as an independent Socialist Party, one phase was over and a new one began.

4

1952-63: Period of Change

I could not attend the Pachmari conference of the Socialist Party (1952), because on the eve of the Pachmari Conference, a delegation of the Socialist Party was sent to Yugoslavia at the invitation of Marshal Tito. Farid Ansari led the delegation, which included Karpoori Thakur, Banke Bihari Das, Mrs Shanti Nayak and myself. After the break with Moscow, Josip Broz Tito and Yugoslavia's government had invited us because we had taken a very sympathetic stand towards Yugoslavia from the beginning after the break.

At the Betul Conference of the Party in 1953, a heated debate took place when Asoka Mehta, the General Secretary, submitted a report in which he had pleaded for political compulsions of a backward economy. He said, "In a backward economy like India, we cannot afford the luxury of Ruling Party and Opposition Party and therefore, the Congress MPs and we (the Socialists) must cooperate". Asoka Mehta was a strong protagonist of the Nehru-JP talks, though Acharya Narendra Deva was not supportive of such cooperation. Jawaharlal Nehru desired to have talks with JP about prospects of cooperation between the Congress and the Praja Socialist Party. JP in consultation with some colleagues prepared the 24-Point Programme that triggered a heated discussion. In fact, there was a division in the Party and Dr. Ram Manohar Lohia strongly led the opposition. JP in his Foreword to Mukut Bihari

Lal's biography of Acharya Narendra Deva said, "I told Asoka Mehta, I did not mind having talks with Jawaharlal Nehru on behalf of the PSP, but I do not theorize by saying that there was a political compulsion of a backward economy for the Congress-PSP cooperation". JP did not agree with Asoka Mehta on that view. While discussing the programme during the talks JP indicated to Jawaharlal Nehru that even if they came to an agreement on the programme he was not eager to join the government. It was wrong to attribute any motives to JP, as some people have tried to. It is clear from what he said in the foreword to Mukut Bihari's book. This stands testimony to the fact that even if the agreement were to succeed, JP was not going to be a part of the government and he would remain on the mass front working in the country for the people's interests. All sorts of motives were attributed to JP at that time and the climate, I must say, was very unhealthy.

Congress-PSP Cooperation

I strongly opposed it. At a later stage, Acharya Narendra Deva in his article on the Congress-PSP cooperation wrote, "I never expected that since ideologically the Congress and the PSP were on different wavelengths this move for cooperation would materialize." This became very clear when Jawaharlal Nehru in his final letter stated that "I do not think time has come for both the parties, the PSP and the Congress to commit to a time-bound Socialist programme. But anyway our good relations should continue".

Earlier, at the Patna Conference of the Socialist Party in 1949, there was another controversy regarding converting the Socialist Party from a cadre-based party to a mass party. An overwhelming majority was in agreement with JP's viewpoint, which favoured a mass party. Formerly we were a cadre party, party of active workers, but then that was to be widened and made a mass party as a part of the democratization process. There it was decided to throw the membership open to the people. Some hardliners led by Ramanandan Mishra campaigned that converting it into a mass party would dilute the revolutionary dynamism of the party. A marathon debate took place. In his remarkable speech JP said, "I am addressing this Conference as a Marxist [till that time he had not given up Marxism] and the Marxist dynamism requires that the base of the party must be widened. Merely because the party is made a mass party, it does not mean that we become tools in the hands of the exploiting classes and dilute our ideology. Ultimately, even if mass membership is allowed, it is the active cadre, which is ideologically oriented, that will dominate the Party and give a thrust to the Party's decisions. Had we remained only a small ideologically oriented cadre Party, we would not have grown in strength in the trade unions, kisan movement, etc. So any party that seeks to pursue a democratic polity has to be a mass party". JP spoke for more than three hours giving an ideological justification of a mass party.

With his profound ideological convictions, he elaborated his views extensively with the delegates listening to him in spellbound silence. I participated in the debate and stoutly defended the ideological orientation about the proposed formation of the mass party. In his speech JP brought forward various facets of Socialism, Marxism, Dialectical Materialism, etc. He discussed the post-Russian Revolution situation and also the structures of social democratic parties in different parts of the world.

In my opinion, JP's intellectual calibre was put to test in this debate. The delegates were deeply impressed by JP's intellectual abilities. Acharya Narendra Deva was also in favour of a mass party. Some hardcore elements that opposed the concept of a mass party were Trotskyites, formerly of the Bolshevik-Leninist Party of India that had merged in the Socialist Party. Also among them was Sheila Pereira, who vigorously led the opposition. The irrepressible spokesman of the opposition to mass party resolution was Ramanandan Mishra from Bihar. You may remember that in 1942, he had escaped from the prison along with JP to join the underground movement. However, the resolution favouring a mass party was passed with overwhelming majority.

Spade, Prison and Vote

JP too believed in the famous slogan coined by Dr. Lohia, 'Spade, Prison and Vote.' It was decided that Dr. Lohia in his Presidential Address at the Pachmari Conference of the Socialist Party should give a new formulation for the Socialist ideology and a top-ranking leader, like JP, should initiate the debate. Accordingly JP initiated the debate on Dr. Lohia's Presidential Address.

The debate at Pachmari provided a refreshing ideological orientation.

There was no division between the leadership and the rank and file. Almost all leaders were together. Even Dr Lohia was a strong protagonist of the mass party idea. Some differences among the leaders, irrespective of the nature of the party, existed even earlier. For instance, on the question of attitude towards the Communists there was a division among the leadership. For years, men like Asoka Mehta, Achyut Patwardhan, Minoo Masani and some others were critical of the Communists. Acharya Narendra Deva and JP were in favour of the Left Consolidation including the Communists. But later on it became clear that the Communists were working against the Socialists and therefore the latter's attitude changed. The position taken by Communists during the war ('People's War') and their role during the 1942 struggle hastened the break-up in the relationship between the Communists and the Socialists.

Firing in Travancore-Cochin

At a later stage, some serious differences emerged on certain issues. A bitter controversy took place on the issue of the firing in Travancore-Cochin during the PSP regime in Kerala and sowed the seeds of division in the party. I personally felt that we were near a split. Dr Lohia, of course, took a very strong view. He was the General Secretary of the Party when he was in jail. He sent a telegram to Pattom Thanu Pillai, Chief Minister of Kerala, urging him to appoint a judicial enquiry into the police firing and simultaneously tender the resignation of his ministry. Then the National Executive Committee of the PSP went through the matter carefully. It passed an unusual resolution taking the moral responsibility of the episode and tendering its apologies to the nation. The resolution stated, "We have failed to formulate a code of conduct for a Socialist government in handling the problems of law and order. So, it is really a failure of the entire movement and the National Executive and we share the blame".

Generally in such a situation appointing a commission to look into the matter and bringing out a report would have provided the solution. A commission was appointed to enquire into the police firing. However, Dr Lohia wanted that the ministry should first resign, before the inquiry could begin. Though the National Executive's resolution was passed in the Conference by majority vote, supporters of Dr Lohia's views were thoroughly dissatisfied. This division gradually led to the split in the PSP.

I voted for the balanced resolution of the National Executive of the Praja Socialist Party. The demand for immediate resignation of the Ministry was an extreme approach. The National Executive's resolution had both a moral and a realistic content. Anyway, JP spoke very eloquently in the General Council meeting of the Party at Nagpur where the National Executive's balanced resolution was passed. Dr Lohia, Madhu Limaye and others were not satisfied with the draft resolution prepared by the National Executive of the PSP.

Unification with KMPP

The issue, on which the Socialist leadership was somewhat divided, was on the merger of the Kisan Mazdoor Praja Party (KMPP) and the Socialist Party. A major section of the leadership was on one side, but Acharya Narendra Dev had a different opinion. Ultimately the Socialist Party became the Praja Socialist Party (PSP) by merging the Socialist Party, Kisan Mazdoor Praja Party and Forward Bloc (Subhas). Leaders like Dr Lohia, Asoka Mehta and JP, felt that it was a logical culmination of the Pachmari Resolution, which had talked of political consolidation in the country against the then regime of the Congress.

I was totally opposed to the merger and in the National General Council meeting, held at Bombay, I made a very strong speech against the merger. I expressed the view that we were destroying our ideological moorings. I pointed out, "Acharya Kripalani feels that party needs only a programme and not a social philosophy or an ideology. I am totally opposed to this perspective." But ultimately Acharya Narendra Deva, who presided over the General Council meeting, made an impassionate plea to the leadership. He had three main concerns about the merger, First, he was concerned that the merger would lead to dilution of party's commitment to organizing struggles; second, he did not agree with the view expressed by the KMPP that for a party there is no need of a social philosophy and ideology; and thirdly, he did not feel Acharya Kripalani was committed to Socialism at all. He was presiding over the meeting. After expressing his concerns about the merger Narendra Dev proceeded, "Every member sitting here in the Council knows my views against the proposed merger. But I take cognizance of the reality that almost the entire leadership of the party, JP, Dr Lohia, Asoka Mehta, Madhu Limaye, and others have already moved the process of merger ahead. The talks have taken place and unification of the KMPP and the Socialist Party has almost become a fait accompli. Many of you have expressed your views against the merger and my views are also with you. However, under the current circumstances, we should not split the party on this issue. We should go ahead with the merger." His concluding remarks provided an anti-climax to his earlier criticism. The split in the party was averted.

Allahabad Perspective

The next PSP Conference was at Allahabad. The Allahabad Document totally rejected the Congress – PSP cooperation and so the controversy ended.

At the Allahabad Conference, Acharya Narendra Dev made a memorable speech. With a sense of humour and sarcasm, he said, "Merely to expand should not be the vision of the party; to deepen our policy and ideology should be our concern". And then he said, "We are meeting at Allahabad where there is confluence of the Ganga, the Jamuna and the Saraswati. I would like our party leaders and members to realize that just as at Allahabad, we have got the confluence of three rivers, the Socialist Party, the KMPP and the Forward Bloc (Subhas). In the merger of rivers at Allahabad, the Saraswati has remained dormant but the Socialist stream in this merger should not become dormant. Some of those who are for mere expansion may want the Party bigger. We might think in terms of bringing in the Congress also. The Congress is like an ocean. It is vast, but there are also crocodiles inside and the water is salty.

So, please be careful. Let us stop here! Let us not go still further (an alliance with Congress) merely to expand the party."

So, the Allahabad policy statement was very clear. It had welcomed whatever had taken place, but there was no question of forging an alliance with the Congress. The controversy ended. Asoka Mehta's membership was terminated when he accepted the Deputy Chairmanship of the Planning Commission and joined the Government's United Nations Delegation because the party was opposed to that. In the National Executive meeting in Bombay. Prem Bhasin and I pointed this out to Mehta and told him it was time for us to part. Asoka Mehta's cryptic reply was "I won't oblige the party by resigning". A resolution was passed terminating his membership. It was painful but was an inevitable decision.

Asoka Mehta's Return

Asoka Mehta joined the Congress at the request of the Congress President Kamaraj and supported Indira Gandhi. When the Emergency was declared, strangely enough Asoka Mehta and I were in the same cell in Rohtak Jail. One night I found Asoka restless, tossing in his bed. When I asked him, "Are you disturbed?", he said "I am not disturbed because I have lost my sleep. I am not concerned about my disturbed sleep. I am worried about my shattered dreams". Then he said, "I tried to persuade you young people, that you should join the Congress and I thought Indira Gandhi could be a strong force. But I realize that she has betrayed not only me, but betrayed the nation and betrayed democracy also. You can be assured that after passing this circuitous path, now I will be with you and up to my end I will remain with you". Then, the Congress broke up. After going through the formation of Congress (O) he finally helped in forming the Janata Party and was with us till his death. He was appreciative of the work that some of us were doing in Parliament and outside. I was happy that Asoka Mehta who brought me into Socialist politics in Bombay again became my senior colleague and leader.

JP had once been asked at a Bombay meeting whether they wanted Acharya Narendra Deva or him to be the President of the Congress as desired even by Mahatma Gandhi. But the reality of the situation was that most of the Congress leaders would not allow that to happen. After the 1942 struggle Mahatma Gandhi had said (as also reported by the Press at that time) that in order to see that young elements were integrated into the Congress, people like JP and Acharyaji who reflected the mood of the country in the post 1942 era, could be made President. Almost the entire leadership of the Congress, except Mahatma Gandhi, rejected the suggestion. Even Jawaharlal Nehru did not favour the proposal.

Exit from Congress a blunder?

Against the background of India's partition and the assassination of Mahatma Gandhi, Dr Ram Manohar Lohia was of the opinion that it was not the appropriate time to leave the Congress. JP and Acharya Narendra Dev were of the same opinion. It was surprising to learn that Asoka Mehta was of the opinion that the party must quit the Congress. After JP and Lohia ascertained the views of the rank and file, they too agreed with the proposal to leave the Congress, and did not consider exit from the Congress a blunder.

It is a strange dialectic that Mehta, who later on went to the Congress, was taking the anti-Congress stand before 1948!

Attitude Towards Nehru

Dr Lohia and to some extent JP were very close to Jawaharlal Nehru initially when we were inside the Congress, Dr. Lohia was appointed Secretary-in-Charge of the International Department of the AICC. Jawaharlal Nehru had a close relationship with Acharya Narendra Deva. They were together in the Ahmednagar Fort prison during the Quit India movement. While Jawaharlal Nehru wrote the famous book *The Discovery of India* during his time in the jail, Acharya Narendra Deva and Maulana Azad were also detained in the same jail. I was present at a Press conference addressed by Jawaharlal Nehru after his release. He was asked a question, "You wrote *The Discovery of India* but you had no sources inside the jail for reference!" Jawaharlal Nehru said, " Of course, I had no references in the form of books, but I had two living encyclopedias with me, Acharya Narendra Dev and... Maulana Abul Kalam Azad".

I have quoted this to illustrate the emotional bond among these veterans.

The Chinese aggression

We were very critical of Jawaharlal Nehru and Krishna Menon, the Defence Minister. I remember, during the days of the Chinese aggression, when the meeting of the Congress Parliamentary Party was in session, there was a clamour in the Congress Parliamentary Party that the Defence Minister Krishna Menon should resign. Jawaharlal Nehru got up and said, "Krishna Menon is only implementing what I believe, and is giving expression to my policy. If you want him to resign, demand my resignation also". Mahavir Tyagi, an articulate Congress MP, got up and said, "If you say that, then as one among those who have elected you as the Leader of our Parliamentary Party, I demand that you should resign." There was panic in the meeting. Several Congress MPs went to Tyagi's seat and remonstrated. Jawaharlal Nehru shouted from the chair, "Don't worry, don't try to pacify him; we are good friends." This incident reflects how the Congressmen in those days were not just trumpet blowers of leaders but were people who gave articulate expression to their views and criticism in the face of grave national crisis.

5

Goa Liberation Struggle

In one of the meetings held at Pune, Acharya Kripalani had observed that in addition to individual batches of satyagrahis there should be a mass satyagraha for the liberation of Goa and therefore the Goa Vimochan Sahayak Samiti (Goa Liberation Aid Committee) was formed. It was called the Goa Vimochan Sahayak Samiti because basically the Goa National Congress was conducting the movement for several years and we took the role of assisting them. The Goa Liberation Aid Committee or the Goa Vimochan Sahayak Samiti decided that on 15 August 1955, we would offer mass satyagraha in Goa by sending large number of volunteers from various parts of India to the Goa border to defy the ban on entry into Goa.

I was Secretary of the Goa Vimochan Sahayak Samiti in Bombay and we had mobilized a lot of support. On 13 August 1955 along with 1,200 satyagrahis we started by train from Victoria Terminus Station, Bombay, for Belgaum. On our arrival at Belgaum it was decided that we should go to Sawantwadi by buses since the border of Goa is very close to Sawantwadi. Many others from different parts, who participated in the satyagraha, had reached there earlier, so they could go to the border of Goa at Banda. Due to insufficient time our group reached Belgaum Station on 14 August 1955 by train at about 11 o'clock. Then we learnt that the Bombay State

Government had banned any transport of satyagrahis to the border. Naturally it was not possible to reach the Goa border in time for satyagraha on 15 August 1955. As the leader of a group of 1,200 people, I refused to return and decided to go marching. Despite the heavy downpour across the ghats we continued walking. We had to walk 85 miles. We took rest at night and ate rotis and some chutney that people brought for us on the way. On arriving at Sawantwadi, we learned that the satyagraha had already taken place on 15 August in the morning at Banda resulting in firing by Portuguese police in which there were some deaths and injuries to several satyagrahis. As the Goa Vimochan Sahayak Samiti was chalking out the next plan of action I insisted on being allowed to proceed. Mass satyagraha on the border was already suspended for a while since some satyagrahis were shot. Leaders of the Goa Liberation Aid Committee feared that after this firing, if people continued to defy the Portuguese government of Goa, there could be more repression. We decided to move ahead irrespective of the consequences. Ninety-three satyagrahis out of 1,200 were selected to launch satyagraha from the Netarda border on 19 August 1955.

One of the considerations for selection was that the Committee did not want a mass of satyagrahis across the border again. The second determining factor was the willingness of the volunteers to offer satyagraha.

My wife Pramila also came to the Goa border. She insisted that she should be allowed to join the satyagrahis. However the leaders felt that the Portuguese police may subject women to atrocities and so they did not want any woman to go in this batch of ninety-three.

The Committee also thought that the Portuguese would be more frustrated and enraged because we were defying both our own state government and the Portuguese government. Pramila said, "Happen what may, but I am prepared for the consequences! Even if I die, let me die along with other satyagrahis! It does not matter".

One Mrs Indumati Kelkar wanted to participate in the satyagraha but she was also not allowed. I have a book containing the photograph at the Netarda border where Nath Pai and Pramila had come to see us off for the satyagraha.

Earlier women had participated in small groups in the satyagraha. Sudhatai Joshi, the President of the Goa National Congress, offered satyagraha. She was jailed along with Sindhu Deshpande who was arrested and detained in Goa jail.

There is a small village on the border of Goa, called Netarda (seven miles from Banda) and therefore our satyagraha was called the Netarda Satyagraha. We had to walk a lot. We reached our destination by evening of 19 August 1955. Normally when the satyagraha was announced the police were posted on the border but we walked about 7-8 miles beyond the Portuguese border, raising slogans. I had the national tri-colour flag in my hand.

The Portuguese police came. They were well armed. We were stopped. I was in the front and was asked to hand over the flag. I refused to do so. We had come here to hoist this flag in the Goan territory, and I would not surrender it. They beat me and after an intense struggle they took away the flag. We were asked to return but we did not budge.

Our first slogan on *satyagraha* was, *Nahin, nahin, kabhi nahin, Bharat Goa alag nahin.* The second slogan was: *Lathi, goli khayenge, phir bhi Goa jayenge.* That slogan was very dominant.

Assault on Satyagrahis

After 25 minutes or so, the police ordered us to disperse and began a *lathi* charge on all the satyagrahis. When they started beating me, one of my colleagues Vasant Dali held his hand against the lathi. They were beating us with the butts of their rifles and his wrist got fractured. The police started beating people and were leading them towards the Indian border – but I did not move. They beat me till I fell unconscious. Strangely enough, even after I became unconscious, they trampled on my back with their military shoes. After a while, my colleagues took me to Military Hospital at Belgaum and then to Bombay. They found that my hip joints were injured very badly and I had to be given infrared rays for that injury. My strong young bones could take the torture then, but later on after many years it was diagnosed that my hip joints had totally degenerated and replacement of those joints with metallic plates and rods was the only solution. At present I have two stainless steel plates and two metallic rods in my body. In a lighter vein I tell my colleagues that I am not only a man of steel, but also a man of stainless steel.

I remember, the names of all the four persons who carried me in a stretcher up to the border. One of them was Keshav Gore, husband of Mrinal Gore, the second was Dinakar Sakrikar, the third was Baburao Samant, and the fourth was one of our workers, Babu Mumbarkar. All the four were my colleagues in the Socialist movement. The Goa satyagraha was really a very brutal episode as far as police action is concerned. It was not like an individual satyagraha wherein police just arrested the satyagrahis and took them to jail.

Now when people ask, "What was the impact of this satyagraha?" I feel proud to say that it did generate a climate to pressurize the Indian government leading to the military action to liberate Goa. There was hardly any resistance during the military action. My feeling is if this military action had been taken earlier, there would not have been so much of sacrifice and deaths. Our satyagraha in 1955 did create a spirit of resistance against the Portuguese rule in Goa.

As I said earlier, prior to mass satyagraha there was satyagraha by various small groups entering Goa from various points. The leaders of some groups were detained, tried and given heavy sentences. Among the satyagrahis detained and later sentenced by Military Court were N.G. Goray, Shirubhau Limaye, Madhu Limaye, Ishwarbhai Desai, Tridib Choudhary, Jagannath Rao Joshi, Sudhatai Joshi and many others.

The purpose of the satyagraha was to pressurize the Portuguese as well as the Indian governments. Representatives of the Indian government and Jawaharlal Nehru were hesitant. On 15 August, while our mass satyagraha was on, Nehru, in his Independence Day address stated "My heart goes to the Goa border where our Indian citizens are offering satyagraha…." But he did not announce any action. However, public opinion did affect him and his government. Several newspaper editors wrote, " Time has come for action. Why sacrifice these people through satyagraha?" Ultimately the government was compelled to decide to take military action. Therefore, the Goa satyagraha was in a way a catalytic action. The satyagrahis who were given long-term sentences, including the prominent leaders were released. The struggle ended when military action took place and the liberation of Goa became a reality.

Another name that I must mention is Nath Pai. He was the President of the International Union of Socialist Youth and carried on a campaign in Europe for extending support to the Goa struggle against the Portuguese. The freedom fighters in Goa can never forget the glorious role he played. Dr. Ram Manohar Lohia is rightly hailed as the father of Goa liberation for rekindling the liberation struggle through his satyagraha in Goa on the 18th June 1946. People from other parties also participated. Communist leaders, Comrade Chitale, and Nityanand Saha who was shot dead, participated in the struggle. Jagannathrao Joshi who was sentenced, was from the Bharatiya Jan Sangh. However the Socialist participation in Goa's struggle was most pronounced.

6

Samyukta Maharashtra Movement

When the States Reorganization Commission report was released, it became clear that Bombay would not be a part of Maharashtra State. Many of us felt that the reorganization of States should be on linguistic basis subject to geographical continuity and economic viability. During the freedom struggle, Mahatma Gandhi had made a commitment to the nation that the reorganization of the States should be done on the basis of linguistic principles. He emphasized that whatever was the language of the people, should be the language of that State. When people found that the prospect of such reorganization was being subverted, mass demonstrations were held in front of the Assembly. The prominent leader of the Samyukta Maharashtra movement was Shri S.M. Joshi. A huge crowd had assembled at the Flora Fountain and the police resorted to ruthless firing. In the course of the entire Samyukta Maharashtra movement, which was actually sparked off by this event, 105 people were killed. The Flora Fountain (which is now called Hutatma Chowk or Martyrs' Plaza) was the starting point of the agitation. Thereafter it was decided that we should organize satyagraha so that the agitation could be channeled peacefully.

Prominent leaders like Senapati Bapat and Acharya P.K. Atre and members of trade unions joined us at the first satyagraha. We were all arrested and kept in Byculla Central Jail in Bombay. That was just the beginning.

During this period we faced another controversy. The campaign for Samyukta Maharashtra was launched originally under the leadership of Shankarrao Deo, an eminent Congressman and a member of the Congress Working Committee. He was campaigning for Samyukta Maharashtra on the basis of the principle of linguistic organization of States. The Samyukta Maharashtra Parishad, the organization that was originally representing the cause of lingustic states also included other members of the Congress party. The Congressmen within the Parishad realized that there would be a conflict of interests, if the Samyukta Maharashtra Parishad were to launch a movement and confront the central government run by their own party. The prospects of a popular upsurge created an embarrassing situation for the Congressmen within the Samyukta Maharashtra Parishad. Therefore the non-Congress opposition parties decided to change the name of Samyukta Maharashtra Parishad to Samyukta Maharashtra Samiti, with a broad representation from opposition parties and independents.

In the course of the Samyukta Maharashtra movement some leaders were detained in the jails. Despite the arrests our struggle continued and batches of satyagrahis were being sent to court arrest. S.M. Joshi was made President of the Samyukta Maharashtra Samiti. My wife, my brothers and I were put in jails at different times. Initially, some violence had taken place in Bombay but with the formation of Samyukta Maharashtra Samiti and its peaceful satyagraha there was a new tone and temper in our movement. Under the sponsorship of the Samyukta Maharashtra Samiti, we fought the Bombay Municipal Corporation elections. We won by a majority at this election. Subsequently, we also fought Assembly elections and got a substantial number of seats. The largest political group recognized in the Assembly was the Praja Socialist Party. The parties who were a part of the Samiti included the Communists, the Peasants' and Workers' Party and the Praja Socialist Party. We were in a strong and effective position both in Lok Sabha and in the Legislative Assembly even though we were in the opposition.

My Priorities

I was the Secretary of the Samyukta Maharashtra Samiti in Bombay and I was very active. Contesting the election on behalf of the Samiti meant getting elected and focusing on activities inside the legislature. My first preference at that time was organizational work, constructive activities, planning struggle programmes, and training youngsters. I was conducting study classes and so I did not voluntarily contest. However I was involved in intense organizational functions and campaigning during those elections in 1957.

With the demand of separate States of Gujarat and Maharashtra the animosity between the Gujarati and Marathi population in Bombay almost disappeared and the Samiti sent batches of satyagrahis from Maharashtra to Ahmedabad to support the Maha Gujarat movement. Gujarat meanwhile realized that it was better to have a separate State of its own called 'Maha Gujarat'.

As I have already said, during the early phase of the Samyukta Maharashtra movement some violence did take place. However, later on it was curbed. Near the office of the Praja Socialist Party in Bombay there was a 'Vanguard Studio' owned by Gujarati gentleman. One day some rabid elements went to attack that studio. I stood in front of the studio and told the miscreants, "First you will have to finish me and then you can destroy this studio." The fact that I was an activist of the Samyukta Maharashtra movement and yet was protecting the Gujrati gentleman's studio had an electrifying effect and they went away. The proprietor of the studio thanked me profusely. I replied, "You need not thank me. I have only followed the avowed policy of the Samyukta Maharashtra Samiti, which believed in a peaceful movement without hatred against any linguistic group."

Initially a section of the Gujarati population in Bombay was afraid that the movement might turn against them. But the Samiti leader S.M. Joshi, along with some of his colleagues, tried a unique experiment during that anxious period. They started staying with the Gujarati families in their chawls. S.M. Joshi was determined to use Gandhian methods to run the movement. He said, "I am an activist of the Samyukta Maharashtra movement; I am the Samiti General Secretary. I am coming here with Gujarati and Marathi friends and we will stay with you at night in some of the disturbed areas to create confidence in you and ensure your safety." It had a positive impact on the Gujarati population. They felt that leaders of the Samyukta Maharashtra movement were conscious that this movement must not go against the linguistic minorities in the city of Bombay. The Centre felt that it should review its decision about the Samyukta Maharashtra movement when the electoral results of the Bombay Municipal Corporation showed that the Corporation had slipped out of the hands of the Congress and the Samiti established its hegemony in the corporation.

C.D. Deshmukh's resignation

The event that gave a lot of moral impetus to the Samyukta Maharashtra movement was when Mr. C.D. Deshmukh, who was then the Finance Minister of India, resigned from the Union Cabinet in protest when he realized that the popular demand for Samyukta Maharashtra was not being considered by the Congress government at the Centre because there appeared to be animus against the Marathi-speaking population. People acknowledged this gesture of Mr. Deshmukh as an example of Gandhian values. It gave a new impetus to the movement. His resignation became an example of how individual sacrifice could have a bigger impact than violence. Later on, Mr. Deshmukh refused the offer to contest elections under the auspices of the Samyukta Maharashtra Samiti. He said, "It is the cause that is important. Politicians will do their duty. I have fulfilled my moral duty." All these sacrifices ultimately culminated in the formation of Samyukta Maharashtra. With the formation of Samyukta Maharashtra, there was a fear that industries would move out of Bombay. The fear was unsubstantiated.

Fortunately at that time all sections were united to achieve the Samyukta Maharashtra. When Prime Minister Jawaharlal Nehru came to Maharashtra to inaugurate the installation of Chhatrapati Shivaji Maharaj's statue at Pratapgarh, S.M. Joshi, the leader of the Samyukta Maharashtra movement, suggested that people should demonstrate before the Prime Minister to reaffirm people's commitment to their causes. On that occasion, I remember, the leaders of Rashtriya Swayamsevak Sangh (RSS) made a statement to the effect that there should be no demonstrations before the Prime Minister when he came to inaugurate the statue of Shivaji. On this issue the RSS was completely isolated. However, as far as the movement is concerned, all the parties participated in a non-partisan spirit. The Communists and those who today believe in a *Hindu* nation also participated, though as a marginal force. The Samyukta Maharashtra movement was a non-partisan movement like the Goa liberation movement.

JP's support

Jayaprakash Narayan issued a statement, when he visited Bombay. Without reservations he lent his support to the cause of the Samyukta Maharashtra with Bombay as its capital. He emphasized that the movement for Samyukta Maharashtra should eschew violence and should assure linguistic minorities that there would be no danger to their lives and property in the new State of Maharashtra. Acharya Narendra Dev, in the National Executive meeting of the Praja Socialist Party, said, "Some people say that the demand for a linguistic state is an expression of tribalism." He emphasized that, "It was the expression of the urges of the people at the grass-root level to ensure that administration and assembly work was carried on in the language of the people." He pointed out that during India's freedom struggle, under the leadership of Mahatma Gandhi, the Congress had made an unequivocal commitment to the principle of linguistic States.

Later, during the Chinese aggression of India, the Communist stance on the aggression created bitter controversy in the Samiti. However, the Socialist leader S.M. Joshi made it clear that there would be no compromise on the question of Chinese aggression and India's sovereignty.

7

Land Liberation Struggle

In the earlier period of the Socialist movement, the major strength of the Socialists came from the peasant movement in places like Bihar and U.P. Huge demonstrations were led by Acharya Narendra Deva, JP and Dr Lohia. Janwani march in front of the Rashtrapati Bhawan and other struggles were conducted. The core membership of the Socialist party really was the working class and the peasantry. Therefore, we felt that the land problem had to be focused. We started the land liberation movement. There were plots occupied by industrialists, which were not being used for industrial production nor were these plots available to the tenants or poor people for housing. A similar situation existed in rural areas. Therefore the United Socialist Movement organized satyagraha to demand land liberation in 1969. Many of us were jailed. We supported and highlighted the issue of making land available to the poor in urban and rural areas. I participated in this movement.

Intensification of Struggles

In 1952, the foodgrain prices had risen enormously. Karpoori Thakur, Banke Bihari Das, Shanti Nayak and I were in Yugoslavia. At that time an extensive anti-price rise satyagraha was organized in Bombay and all over Maharashtra. Each elected Municipal Corporator in Bombay was directed to lead a satyagraha in his/her respective constituency and court arrest. We had a strong organization in Bombay called Mill Mazdoor Sabha. The work of Mill Mazdoor Sabha was not limited to only pursuing the demands of individual factories and mills. It mobilized the entire textile industry. The Socialists led the famous textile strike in Bombay for two and a half months on the issue of 'bonus' for textile workers. During this strike, the Socialists popularized the concept that 'bonus' was not just an 'ex-gratia' payment to be made at the mercy of the employer, but a 'deferred wage' that must fill up the gap between the 'living wage' and the 'real wage'. In those days, the Socialists held important positions and gained strength in the trade unions of Railways, Dock and Transport, Textiles, BEST and several middle class employees' unions. JP and Asoka Mehta were the prominent leaders of the trade union movement.

The Communists were not very active excepting in select areas in the Thane district where Godavari Parulekar led the Warlis and Adivasis. She had built up a very strong movement and formed an organization of Adivasis in Telengana as well. The Communists were well organized particularly in Andhra Pradesh and Kerala.

The decline of the Socialist Party on the one hand and of the Communist Party on the other, led to the weakening of overall struggles of the working class and the peasantry to a great extent. During this period the biggest Kisan satyagraha was the Pardi Satyagraha in Gujarat, led by Asoka Mehta and Ishhwarbhai Desai. Socialists were in the forefront of all the struggles on various issues facing the peasants, consumers, or industrial workers. They focused on issues of bonus for workers and the hardships faced by the landless poor.

These struggles contributed a lot to improve the condition of the poor peasantry, labourers and workers. Certain concepts came to stay only as a result of this intensified pressure through such struggles.

8

Cooperative Movement

Vaikunthbhai Mehta was once the Finance Minister of Bombay state. He was a Gandhian and did not want to enter the legislature. Many other Gandhians advised him that a man of his character would be able to change the complete profile of the finance ministry. He accepted the advice. Vaikunthbhai was deeply interested in the Cooperative movement and not as much in the Finance Ministry, which he headed around the same time

Dr D.R. Gadgil, the former Deputy Chairman of the Planning Commission of the Government of India, also shared Vaikunthbhai's commitment to the Cooperative movement. They believed that unless a strong cooperative base was built in the country, the power would be concentrated at the top in Delhi and the process of decentralization would get a setback. Together they had created the great ethos of the cooperative movement in those days.

During that time, along with the peasant movement, the working class movement and the anti-price rise movement, the Cooperative movement too received appreciable momentum. The city of Mumbai in which I was working for a long time had a history in this direction. I am very proud that some of our colleagues and friends in the 1942 movement undertook the task of organizing an ideal cooperative in the areas where working class people lived. Today these cooperatives are called 'Apna Bazar' and branches of

'Apna Bazar' are located in different parts of Maharashtra. Our colleagues in the Socialist movement developed the cooperatives and today the concept of 'Apna Bazar' has been very successful.

Multifaceted Cooperation

The Co-operative Movement was not restricted only to the consumers' field but it also spread to the housing, credit and banking, sugar, powerloom, handloom as well as *Khadi* and village industry sectors. The Cooperatives are also formed by women and adivasis. I am proud that some of my dedicated colleagues are actively associated with these cooperative activities.

Several countries have shown that where healthy cooperative movements exist in different fields, the movement has immensely contributed towards building an egalitarian society. This social context of the cooperative movement is most significant.

9

Electoral Politics

I had a very short stint in the Maharashtra Legislative Council. In 1970 the graduate voters elected me to the Maharashtra Legislative Council, directly from the Bombay Graduates Constituency. The graduates' constituency comprised the residents of Bombay, who had a college degree and had enrolled themselves as voters for the Legislative Council election. The election is conducted by a preferential vote system. Just one month before the elections the party asked me to contest the seat that had to be won, and I did win. However, I was able to perform my duties as a Legislative Council member for less than a year.

Entry in Parlament

Lok Sabha elections were declared in 1971. My giving up the Legislative Council membership to contest the Lok Sabha election was quite accidental. Just one month prior to the Lok Sabha elections, Nath Pai, our sitting Member of Parliament from Rajapur, died of a heart attack. He represented the Rajapur constituency of Maharashtra in the Lok Sabha in 1957, 1962 and 1967. Rajapur was considered a stronghold of the Socialists. All our party workers asked me to contest the Lok Sabha election from Rajapur. I declined saying, "I want to concentrate on the organizational work in Bombay and would not like to seek Lok Sabha election." The veteran

Socialist leader N.G. Goray insisted that in order to retain that constituency it was necessary for me to contest. I had to come around to the majority point of view in the party and agreed to contest. Very little time was available for preparations and campaign. We had only one month. Maharashtra had 48 Lok Sabha seats in 1971. Well, we faced two major challenges at that time. On one side, there was an upsurge of popular sentiment for Prime Minister Indira Gandhi as a result of India's victory against Pakistan and the formation of Bangladesh. On the other hand, the Congress party had nominated the son of Sawantwadi's Maharaja as my opponent. One of the reasons why Barrister Nath Pai's heart trouble precipitated was that he was disgusted by the fact that a person from a feudal background was brought into the democratic polity to fight him. He expressed his anger in the words, "They (Congress party) talk about Socialism and they want to put a princely candidate against me. What type of Socialism is this?" The election resulted in the Congress party winning 47 seats in Maharashtra. The Opposition won only one seat and that was mine. I won five Lok Sabha elections consecutively from the Rajapur constituency in the Konkan region of Maharashtra in 1970, 1977, 1980, 1984 and 1989. In 1980 I won with the highest percentage vote difference in the country. I polled 74 per cent of the total valid votes polled in the Lok Sabha constituency defeating the Congress candidate who secured only 26 per cent votes.

My associations with organized trade unions, cultural organizations, friends in various professions and my former students helped me substantially. I owe a debt of gratitude to them and I am proud that I did not resort to any financial malpractices to raise funds for my elections.

I was in the Maharashtra Legislative Council for a very short time, since I had to resign from the Council when I was elected to the Lok Sabha in 1971. I dealt with the problems of peasantry in general and particularly the issue of land distribution and the problems of the working class in the Council. When elected to the Lok Sabha in 1971 I raised the issue of bonus for the workers. I had moved a Private Member's Bill seeking reconsideration of the concept of bonus as a deferred wage in 1971, when R.K. Khadilkar was the Union Labour Minister. I took an ideological stand that we did not want bonus to be considered a favour bestowed on the workers by the owners of the means of production.

During that period I had to continually represent the issues arising out of the textile strike. Various aspects of the Land Liberation movement were keenly debated in the legislature. The city of Bombay faced an acute scarcity of housing. To bring focus on this problem we adopted a novel idea. Near Worli area of Bombay there was a building called the 'Gwalior Palace'. We took a number of poor families from the surrounding hutments to the 'Gwalior Palace' and symbolically occupied it. It was a new form of satyagraha. We were arrested. The hutment dwellers were sentenced to 15 days' imprisonment and leaders were sentenced to imprisonment for one month. The issue of rehabilitation of the homeless received wide publicity and received the needed attention.

The land liberation issue was important, both for rural areas as well as for urban areas where land was grabbed by a small group of rich individuals and as a result was not available to the poor for affordable housing. Land was allotted to or snatched away by the rich whenever it was available, so we organized satyagrahas at the site. It was called the Land Liberation movement. In the course of this movement, many of us went to jail. In those old days, whenever economic or social issues arose, people were prepared to fight and ultimately the government was forced to respond in some measure.

I will give you a concrete example. Sane Guruji was not a formal member of our Socialist Party, but we always gave our unstinted support to him. He was a personality renowned in Maharashtra's social and political movements. He led the well-known Satyagraha at Pandharpur, a holy place in Maharashtra, with the demand that the so-called lower castes (dalits) be provided access to the temple. Some Congressmen wrote to Mahatma Gandhi that Sane Guruji was taking an extremist view and that his agitation would provoke violence by orthodox people. Mahatma Gandhi wrote to Sane Guruji with a request that he should give up his plans for a fast unto death and wait for the settlement of the problem through persuasion. Sane Guruji wrote back to Mahatma Gandhi, "Bapuji I have the highest regards for you. You have given your advice on this issue but it seems that it is based on wrong reports. Therefore, I will go ahead." On the advice of eminent leaders like Senapati Bapat, and S.M. Joshi, the only compromise accepted by Sane Guruji was that before he commenced his fast, he would first mobilize public opinion through a tour of different districts of Maharashtra along with a cultural troupe that would propagate the message of social equality. Ultimately temple priests realized that public opinion was strongly in favour of opening the doors of the famous Pandharpur temple to dalits. It was a triumph for Sane Guruji and the cause of equality, which he espoused.

In 1952, a number of Municipal Corporators from the Praja Socialist Party in Bombay organized a satyagraha on the issue of rising prices. Every corporator who was elected on a party ticket had to lead a big procession of satyagrahis in his or her respective constituency. The problem of rising prices was not fully solved but a climate of protest was created, and it helped in securing some relief to the consumers.

In those days, there was a greater awareness and commitment to people's genuine issues, which is lacking today.

Assistance from Artistes

Prithviraj Kapoor, the veteran actor, who migrated from Punjab province, played a remarkable role in Bombay. He produced Hindi plays under the auspices of Prithvi Theatres. His plays helped create awareness about communal harmony and social problems. Once, when the All-India Congress Committee session was being held in Bombay, members of the AICC were invited to a special performance of *Deewar* (Wall), symbolizing the divide sought to be created between India and Pakistan. At that time, though Pakistan was not created, the demand for creation of Pakistan was in the air and the play was produced as a counter to that atmosphere of division. Prithviraj carried on his campaign of compassion and integration. Subsequent to *Deewar*, he produced a number of plays, which spread the message of humanity, brotherhood, and compassion. Prithviraj Kapoor represented the mental make-up of the Pathans of the North-West Frontier Province through another play called *Pathan*. He helped share a message of integration by bringing people together to see his plays. Each of his plays was a classic.

During the freedom movement another theatre group, 'Indian National Theatre' was formed in Bombay. INT was formed with the blessings of the famous freedom fighter, socialist and artist Kamaladevi Chattopadhyay, Damu Jhaveri and his colleagues.

Role in Parliament

My first speech was a homage to Nath Pai during obituary references. The first Bill on which I had the opportunity to make a significant contribution was the debate on the 24th Constitutional Amendment Bill, which triggered the controversy on the supremacy of Parliament over Judiciary. In the Golak Nath case 1967, the Supreme Court had reversed, by a narrow majority, its own earlier decisions upholding the power of Parliament to amend all parts of the Constitution including Part III relating to fundamental rights. The result of the judgment was that Parliament was considered to have no power to take away or curtail any of the fundamental rights even if it became necessary to do so for the attainment of the objectives set out in the Preamble to the Constitution. The 24th amendment, sought to provide expressly to Parliament the power to amend any part of the Constitution.

In fact we always believed that the Constitution has clearly defined the fields of activities of different institutions. Therefore in my speech at that time in 1971, I said, "People are supreme as far as electing the rulers is concerned. Parliament is supreme in enacting laws and amending the Constitution, but the Supreme Court is supreme in deciding whether the amendments made by Parliament are within the framework of the spirit of the Constitution." I strongly pleaded at that time for Nath Pai's Private Member's Bill accepting the supremacy of the Parliament as far as Constitutional amendments were concerned. As I had raised the issue a number of times, I was ready with all the information required to put forward my point of view. In the very first week I had the opportunity to make a mark in the Parliament. Subsequently, I got many more opportunities to play an important part in Parliament debates. I spent a lot of time in research in the Parliament library to support my speeches with facts and references, though the speeches were delivered ex tempore. The Library in the Parliament is amongst a few libraries around the world where records of the House of Commons are preserved in a database. I have often referred to the Debates of the Constituent Assembly at the Parliament library. The library is also able to provide access to the reference materials from all the State Assemblies. The accessibility of rich reference resource provided me the opportunity to refer to parliamentary precedents from time to time. The Parliament library became a valuable resource for my success in the Parliament during the five consecutive terms (1971, 1977, 1980, 1985, and 1989).

Wars in Sixties

Our jawans played a heroic role in war. The Chinese aggression into Indian territory took place in 1962. Then, there was a direct attack on India by Pakistan in 1965. During the Chinese War and in the Pakistan War I was Secretary of the Citizens' Defence Committee of Bombay. It would be interesting to refer to a public debate that took place during that time, over the issue of entering the enemy territory. The controversy was about whether it was proper on the part of our jawans to enter the Lahore sector in the Pakistani territory. The Socialists pleaded that once India was attacked by any foreign power, India should have the right to determine on which land to fight the aggressor. In the meetings, organized under the auspices of the Citizens' Defence Committee I put forth the view, "Our Indian army is an army of liberation and not an army of occupation. Therefore, if our army has gone to Lahore, it was only a military strategy. The army was allowed to go right up to Lahore. Prime Minister Lal Bahadur Shastri has assured the Socialists that our army is an army of liberation, not of occupation, and whatever does not belong to us, won't be occupied by us after the end of war". Some jingoist and chauvinist elements in the country criticized the withdrawal from Lahore, but we did not agree with their point of view. The correct thing to do was for our army to come back as soon as victory was declared.

Critics of the Simla Agreement say that Indira Gandhi should not have released the prisoners-of-war. I do not think that Indira Gandhi committed a mistake by releasing them and signing the Simla Agreement. The Simla Agreement was signed in a climate of understanding and assistance. Sometimes we judge the events of history in the background of the current circumstances and that is not appropriate. There was nothing wrong in releasing most of the prisoners under the Simla Agreement. The objective was to solve the problem in an amicable manner. I do not think the Simla Agreement created any difficulties for us.

10

Decline of Political Morality

SVD Governments

In the era in Indian politics called the era of non-Congressism, we had heterogeneous SVD governments. The constituents of the SVD governments did not share a common mindset or values nor were they guided by common policies. Our PSP's National Executive discussed this issue, but by majority it was decided that as expediency, we should go in for the SVD governments. However, some of us had recorded our dissent in the minutes of the meeting. Among the dissenters were Prem Bhasin and myself. I believe that SVD governments were the beginning of a phase in Indian politics when value-oriented politics started getting pushed to the background.

Leaders from different parties had contributed to the collapse of political morality. In 1969, Mrs. Indira Gandhi planned the defeat of the official candidate of the Congress, Neelam Sanjeeva Reddy for the Presidential election and helped V.V. Giri to win. She also gained support of some of the opposition parties to ensure the defeat of her own party's candidate. She initially supported the name of Reddy as the official candidate, but then provoked Giri to rebel. Today, some people may describe such behaviour as a political strategy, but for me it signified the beginning of the collapse of political morality in India.

Strategy or Compulsion

What were the compulsions of Indira Gandhi to act in the manner in which she did? Was it simply because of political strategy or were there some hidden reasons as well? She was settling her individual scores inside the Congress Party High Command. Secondly, she had also started feeling that she needed to demonstrate her strength and consolidate her bargaining power within the party. The Presidential election and the election inside the Congress Party were used to turn the tables on her opponents within the party. She continued this process of consolidation of power within her party even after the Presidential election. Indira Gandhi also tried to gain legitimacy within the party and amongst the general masses by espousing causes such as nationalization of banks, abolition of the Privy Purses of princes and certain land reforms. In the meantime she took a firm attitude about Bangladeshis. I do not think that bank nationalization, abolition of privy purses, and other economic policies she pursued at that time, were a result of a social commitment. She wanted to use these actions as a mechanism to counter dissent within her party.

The Socialists had been demanding all these actions long before she implemented them. For many years, we were insisting that privy purses should be abolished. Acharya Kripalani had even termed privy purses given to the former princes as wages of treachery to Indian nationalism.

Finance Minister C.D. Deshmukh was not a Socialist, but he had a pragmatic approach to economic and social problems. When the question of LIC (Life Insurance Corporation) came up for discussion in the Parliament, he was the first in the government, not Mrs. Gandhi, who strongly pleaded for nationalization of the insurance sector and recommended the creation of LIC. He held the view that financial institutions had the potential to build up large resources and surpluses that should be made available for the developmental activities. Surpluses in the hands of the private sector financial institutions would not be available to developmental activities. He questioned why financial institutions should then be in the hands of the private companies? He suggested that the government could establish an organization in the public sector like LIC and give it a mandate that if LIC mopped up surpluses, a certain percentage should be used for developmental activities. The issue of using surpluses for developmental activities never comes up with regard to surpluses generated by engineering or automobile industries. The point is that the financial sector is critical to developmental activities. Years after the formation of the LIC, we find that it has generated vast resources that have been provided to people in many sectors, in rural and other areas through large scale assistance and loans for developmental activities. Therefore, what C.D. Deshmukh had envisioned, proved to be correct.

I do not think that during his time, even Jawaharlal Nehru was very keen on nationalizing life insurance. My point is, Mrs. Gandhi did not nationalize the banks with any ideological motivation or a comprehensive follow-up plan for a social mandate for the nationalized institutions. It was merely a political decision to gain popularity and to checkmate her opponents within the party.

At the Bangalore session of the AICC in 1969, Indira Gandhi scribbled a small note about her plan for bank nationalization and sent it to the AICC. In that note, she wrote, "These are my stray thoughts, hurriedly jotted down." When her ideas were discussed in the AICC, senior leaders of the Congress party like Morarji Desai and Yashwant Rao Chavan said, "There cannot be nationalization without social control and there cannot be social control without nationalization". This is only what they said in support of nationalization. They had not applied their mind properly to the issue. Later on, even Morarjibhai Desai has many times expressed that he did not think that she (Indira Gandhi) had much faith even in nationalization of banks. She only wanted to score a point just as the privy purses were abolished for political expediency. Subsequent events betray the fact that in abolishing the privy purses, she was not committing herself to the principle of abolishing the political power of the erstwhile princely states. Congress party's liaison with the erstwhile royal families continued and many of them became its candidates during subsequent elections. While she made attempts to create an impression in the public mind that she was following socialist policies, in private she remained an opportunist rather than a socialist.

We were not opposed to any individual princely families. The point is that princes represented a particular lobby of vested interest in the country. On their becoming Congress candidates, supporters, or patrons, the image of the party would be compromised. In public life, it is not just what you are but what you appear to be that is important.

I have had the opportunity to talk to Jagjivan Ram several times. There are many people who feel that during the Bangladesh War he was not given his share of credit for the victory. He played a major role in shaping the military strategy as the Defence Minister. However, all the credit was given to Indira Gandhi.

Jagjivan Ram was shrewd enough to gauge people's resentment against the Emergency. Though, he moved the resolution in Parliament when the Emergency was proclaimed, he recognized the popular sentiment against the Emergency when Indira Gandhi, in her nation-wide broadcast, declared that she had advised the President to dissolve the Fifth Lok Sabha and ordered a fresh election. The Opposition leaders were released from jail. We united to form the Janata Party and decided to contest with a common election symbol. Initially there was some hesitation on the part of some parties to merge into a single party. However the statement from JP that he would not take part in the election campaign if a single party was not formed, set the tone for the formation of the Janata Party. Jagjivan Ram, along with Nandini Satpathy and Hemwati Nandan Bahuguna, left the Congress on 2 February 1977 and formed the organization "Congress for Democracy." Soon after the results of the elections were declared they merged with the Janata Party.

Through the period I had known him, I had seen a lot of changes taking place in Morarjibhai, especially in his attitude to political movements. In early years, he appeared to be very rigid in his views on peasant issues and in his responses to movements (such as the Samyukta Maharastra movement). During the Samyukta Maharashtra movement, people considered Morarji Desai a dogged opponent of the movement. He was even perceived by people as an opponent of the demand for a separate Gujarat state. I have heard that Indira Gandhi recognized that there was mass support behind this movement and therefore persuaded her father, Prime

Minister Jawaharlal Nehru, that he should consider the demand. Again I want to stress that even on this issue, she had not applied her mind on the basis of principle, but was merely responding to the political opportunity. Morarjibhai had worked very closely with Indira Gandhi. His contention was that Indira Gandhi was a power-monger. He held the view that once she decided to do something, then she would not worry what means she would adopt to achieve her goal and what consequences would follow. There are always people around leaders who are prepared to oblige. Mrs. Gandhi collected people around her who helped her achieve her goals, without consideration about the means.

Our friends in CPI were very impressed by her actions. Her intention was to put up some sort of a radical Left image and neutralize her opposition. The pro-Communist elements inside the Congress helped strengthen her image during this period.

Her strategy for Bangladesh was planned so meticulously that it pushed the Opposition to the fringe. Nobody could oppose her actions. Her popularity started increasing.

Indira Gandhi had deliberately tried to have links with the CPI. With measures like nationalization of banks, abolition of privy purses, she wanted to create the aura of a radical image around her. No doubt, it helped her to some extent. Now, as far as the abolition of the privy purses is concerned, if I remember right, in the Rajya Sabha, the motion was defeated by a narrow vote.

I will like to mention a very interesting story about Shyam Nandan Mishra, (Congress 'O') who was in the Rajya Sabha. N.G. Goray went to him and said, "Don't vote against this Bill." He voted against it anyway and it was defeated by only a small margin of votes. Shyam Nandan Mishra later told us, "In my constituency I was told that because of my vote, the Bill was defeated."

Though Indira Gandhi tried to create an impression that she believed in socialist ideals, a close observation of her behaviour leads me to say that she neither believed in those ideals nor did she devote enough thinking to some of her radical decisions. Those decisions were made for political expediency. When she realized that anti-Congressism was gaining ground in the country and that six states already had non-Congress governments, she tried to collect some allies, which would give to her a radical image. While some of her decisions gave her temporary advantage, the fact remains that the one-party domination in the Indian political scene was big jolt to democracy.

Decline in Popularity

After 1971 the next election was scheduled for 1976, but by a Constitutional Amendment it was postponed by another year. Indira Gandhi did not want to risk defeat. But in the meantime as ill-luck would have it, a number of scandals came up which created problems for her. The Nagarwala scandal and then the licence scandal became public when L.N. Mishra was the Minister for Foreign Trade.

I have not the least doubt that L.N. Mishra was liquidated. All the railway employees talk about it. So one after another all scandals started pouring in. Corruption also started growing. After seeing all these things, Indira Gandhi felt the sand shifting under her feet.

Around this time, the Congress government introduced a bill for incorporating the Maintenance of Internal Security Act (MISA). When the MISA Bill was put to vote Uma Shankar Dikshit was the Home Minister. In my speech in the Parliament I warned, "When such draconian measures are brought, ostensibly they are brought to deal with anti-social elements and economic offenders. But our experience is that such atrocious legislations are misused against political adversaries." In response Uma Shankar Dikshit got up and said, "Mr. Madhu Dandavate, I can assure the House that this measure will not be utilized against political adversaries". He categorically assured the House that MISA would not be used for political purposes. When I was in jail during the Emergency under the MISA, I did write to him reminding him what we were promised.

Subversion of Values

Look at Indira Gandhi's political evolution. Following the death of her father in May 1964, Indira Gandhi became Minister of Information and Broadcasting in Lal Bahadur Shastri's government. At that time, she would stammer when replying to questions in the Parliament. Dr Lohia and Madhu Limaye used to call her a "goongi gudiya" (a dumb doll). Through time, she pursued her political ambition with determination and emerged as a leader in her own right. There can be no denying of the fact that her ambition for power guided her political actions. This very ambition was reflected in her demanding a conscience vote in the Presidential election, and forcing a split in the Congress party. Indira Gandhi always took risks in her political actions. Many of her actions such as the presidential election of 1969 demonstrated her inclination to gamble with her political career. If her gamble had failed at that time, she would have been thrown into the dustbin of history. But she always took a calculated risk.

Indira Gandhi viewed the concepts of committed bureaucracy and judiciary as weapons to perpetrate her power. I have remained totally opposed to such a view.

Opponent not Enemy

I have followed one principle in my life: 'Even your strongest opponent is not an enemy.' Though I was not the formal Leader of Opposition, I almost functioned like a coordinator for many years. I coordinated meetings of the leaders of various political parties, and helped facilitate and coordinate scathing attacks on the government's anti-people policies. Amongst other issues I was at the forefront of attack on issues related to corruption in the government. For example, I was active in the debate on the notorious Nagarwala scandal. Nagarwala called the State Bank of India and mimicked Prime Minister Indira Gandhi's voice on the phone. He withdrew lakhs of rupees from the State Bank in Parliament Street in New Delhi, pretending that Mrs. Indira Gandhi herself had ordered the withdrawal. I first put the question to the then Finance Minister, Yashwant Rao Chavan. Even when a member of Parliament like me goes to a bank and presents a cheque, the bank verifies from their records whether adequate amount is available. In the Nagarwala case, this gentleman just imitated the voice of Mrs Gandhi and asked for 60 lakh rupees. The money was issued without any questioning or verification. Who is this man who got the money, I asked? There were rumours floating that the money was being sent to Bangladesh. I said that I did not care about such rumours. But the fact remains that he asked for money on the telephone and money was given. Everyone who was involved in that case, including Nagarwala, died one after another and the case became more complicated. I repeatedly challenged the government on the floor of the House and demanded an explanation. The Minister replied, "Do not make allegations if you do not know the facts." I reacted, "What allegations? The fact is that many people associated with this case have died. Lakhs of rupees have been withdrawn from State Bank of India without anybody questioning the bonafides of the person who collected the money. These are the facts. Tell us what really happened." The facts were never revealed because everyone connected with the case died. I fought Mrs. Gandhi's policies and actions relentlessly in the Parliament on principle but I had no personal animosity towards her.

Human Touch

I would like to narrate another interesting episode to illustrate my focus on maintaining a personal relationship with my political opponents. When Indira Gandhi died, I delivered an obituary speech in the Lok Sabha. The full text of my obituary speech on Indira Gandhi is reproduced in a book, *Hundred Best Parliamentary Speeches — 1947-1997*, edited by the former Secretary-General of Lok Sabha, Dr Subhash Kashyap. I started that speech by saying, "Even while offering homage to late Mrs Indira Gandhi, I must make it clear that we did not agree with her on several points, but when a person dies and in Parliamentary life when we rise to pay homage, death takes away many differences and only the points of convergence remain." Then I narrated two-three of my encounters with her. I said, "After she got elected from Chikmagalur constituency and came back to the House, and took oath in Lok Sabha, on that day I was in the Rajya Sabha as a Railway Minister answering questions. That was my day for answering the questions on Railways. During lunchtime, when I was passing through the library corridor, I came across Indira Gandhi. I just looked at her and said, "Oh, Indiraji, congratulations on your victory." She responded, "Hello, Madhu Dandavate, thank you. You have brought distinction to your government. It was my misfortune that you were

not in my cabinet." I said, "Madam, I was fortunate not to be there."
She heartily laughed at my repartee. Then at the end of my obituary
speech I said, "Many have lost many things in this country, when
Smt. Gandhi died. The Congress (I) lost its President. The nation
lost its Prime Minister. Rajiv lost his beloved mother. The Congress
(I) could get back a new President; the nation could get a new
Prime Minister. But Rajiv lost his mother forever. And, therefore,
I pay my homage not only to the former Prime Minister. I am one
among those who believe that all the power of the world can never
be a substitute for a mother's love and affection, and therefore, Sir,
on behalf of the entire House let me give my heartfelt and sincere
condolences to Rajiv Gandhi. Remember that whatever be your
policies and perspectives, it is the indomitable will of your mother
that should be the heritage that you should carry with you." At that
time I noticed that my speech had touched the emotions of the
member parliamentarians and left the women members in the House
sobbing.

Before the beginning of every session of Parliament, there was
a custom that the Opposition leaders met in the Speaker's Chamber
to finalize the agenda for the session. After that there was lunch on
the first floor, which the Prime Minister was to attend. I remember
meeting Rajiv Gandhi during one of the luncheons after Indira
Gandhi's death. Sharad Pawar was also present during this meeting.
In the presence of all members, Rajiv Gandhi said to me, "Professor
Madhu Dandavate, I want to tell you that I was moved by your
speech, as much as I was moved at the time of the death of my
mother." In politics, in spite of tussles, there are humane moments.
I have met Mrs Gandhi a number of times. For instance, whenever
any petitioner came with a problem or a group of marchers came to
demonstrate on an issue and wanted to see Indira Gandhi with their
demands, I would tell her, "Do not ask them to go through the
bureaucrats." Many times I would just call her and say, "These
people have come from Kerala; some have come from the border
areas of Maharashtra; they have a problem, they want to meet you."
Sometimes she would say, "I have no time." And I would say, "No,
Madam, you must find time" On most occasions she would agree
to meet. She was fully aware that despite our differences, I

represented genuine problems and demands of people. She rarely declined my requests. Of course, we will never forget the fact that she kept us in jail for 18 months during the Emergency. I was detained in Bangalore Jail, my wife Pramila in the Yeravada Jail and my brother in the Arthur Road Jail in Mumbai. We were not even allowed to meet. I consider these as aberrations, or inevitable pangs of the perilous political life.

While I was referring to the humane moments of our political life, I must also narrate another anecdote that relates to a humorous exchange between Prime Minister Morarji Desai and me. I had just finished reading a book on Urine Therapy with a foreword written by Morarji Desai. During one of our cabinet meetings, I went over to Morarjibhai and said, "I have to ask you one question. I read one book on Urine Therapy and you have written a Foreword to that book. Do you also practise Urine Therapy?" He said, yes, and "you should also practise it. You will live long." I replied, "Morarjibhai, I want to live long, but with taste." He started laughing.

Parliament vs. Judiciary

I will say something about Nath Pai's Constitution (Amendment) Bill. Nath Pai and I were strong protagonists of the theory that between Parliament and the Judiciary, Parliament was supreme in the matter of amending the Constitution. It is interesting to note that supremacy of Parliament was challenged not by the common people, but by the property owners. In our Constitution, the right to property was earlier included in the List of the Fundamental Rights. The argument given by property holders was that the landlord has property and if you try to bring in land legislations in which you have a ceiling on land and take away the rest of the land above the ceiling for redistribution, you are really disturbing Right to Property. Right to Property was a Fundamental Right and Article 13 (2) says, 'The State shall not make any law which takes away or abridges the rights conferred by this part (Para III on Fundamental Rights) and any law made in contravention of this clause, to the extent of the contravention, will be void.' In two landmark cases, namely Shankari Prasad vs. Union of India and Sajjan Singh vs.

State of Rajasthan, it was ruled that Parliament had the right to amend any part of the Constitution under Article 368 of the Constitution since this amending power is derived from the Constituent Law and not ordinary law to which Article 13 (2) refers in the Constitution. However in the majority judgement in the Golak Nath Case the Supreme Court ruled that taking away property is actually destroying the Right to Property, a fundamental right, in Part III of the Constitution, and according to Article 13(2) the land legislation on ceiling cannot be passed as it would violate the article. Right to Property was since omitted as a Fundamental Right from the Constitution by the (Forty-Fourth) Constitution Amendment Act of 1978.

However in the Kesavananda Bharti judgement of 1973, the Supreme Court ruled that under Article 368, any part of the Constitution could be amended, provided the basic structure of the Constitution was not destroyed. The Supreme Court judgement did not spell out in detail the basic structure, but by way of illustration stated that sovereignty of the country, the nation's unity, the secular character of the State, federalism, adult franchise were some of the key features of the basic structure.

Now I had to revise my attitude. Nath Pai and myself were asking who could bring about the destruction of the Constitution? The British Parliament has said, "Parliament can change everything excepting man to a woman and woman to a man."

Now, to our great disillusionment, during the Emergency, many of us in Parliament were arrested and at that time in our absence, the 42nd Constitutional Amendment was introduced in both the Houses of Parliament. I want to refer to one Amendment which was already passed in the Rajya Sabha. It was a Bill that sought to give immunity from criminal prosecution in normal courts to the Prime Minister, President, Vice-President and the Speaker of Lok Sabha. In effect, what did this mean? If one happens to be a Prime Minister and were to murder someone, in a normal case he or she would face criminal charges. However, he or she would escape the consequences of the criminal act if the Bill were to become a Law. When we read about this Bill in the jail during the Emergency we were shocked. The motivations behind this Bill were too obvious to hide, and an undercurrent of resentment in the public mind was inevitable. Out of guilt, the government did not bring it for adoption in the Lower House. However, some among us in the jail feared that this amendment might be brought back, because it was motivated, in the first place, by an authoritarian regime that clearly wanted to protect itself from the potential excesses of the Emergency period. This act made me think about the issue of the powers of the judiciary versus those of the parliament. I felt that if there were to be no Kesavananda Bharti judgement, probably even the most atrocious 42nd Amendment Bill would have stood the scrutiny of the full Constitutional Bench of the Supreme Court. The only saving grace for all of us, in this context, was that the Kesavananda Bharti judgement says that any amendment of any part of the Constitution is valid so long as it does not violate the basic features of the Constitution.

The Bangladesh War and after

It was not the ruling party, but Indira Gandhi, who took the major credit of the Bangladesh War. Really speaking, both the Defence Minister Jagjivan Ram as well as Indira Gandhi played a very important role. Even in the Central Hall of Parliament, when a reception was given, people congratulated both Indira Gandhi and Babu Jagjivan Ram, but she had an edge. Many old people, who had studied the Defence issues, said that Jagjivan Ram gave her the most appropriate advice. But the credit of victory was given only to Prime Minister Indira Gandhi.

As I revive the memories of the Bangladesh war, I am intensely reminded of the martyrdom of Capt. V.V. Kulkarni, the husband of my youngest sister, Reva, in the Khulna sector.

Later the economic situation deteriorated. The debates in Parliament of that time reflected the situation in the country. I found that after the Bangladesh war a culture of sycophancy spread inside the ruling party. In earlier days if some members of the Congress Party had different views, their opinion would be voiced in both the Parliament and in the Congress Legislative Party. Now, even when people differed, they chose not to voice their thoughts at all. The controversial election of VV Giri as the President of India was a result of the culture of sycophancy.

11

JP's Call for Total Revolution

I have written about Jayaprakash's return to active politics in the 1970's, in my book *JP: Struggle With Values*. At the Sarvodaya Ashram in Bodhgaya in 1954, Jayaprakash Narayan had retired from active politics. The death of Prabhavati Devi, his wife, on 15 April 1973 had a profound impact on JP's future role in Indian politics during the 1970s. JP and Prabhavatiji were soul mates of many years. It would be worth mentioning the conversation between the two after the doctors diagnosed that Prabhavatiji had terminal cancer. On returning home from the doctor's clinic, JP told Prabhavati, "Prabha, I thought that I will be the first to go from this world, but you will have to go first because the doctor has pronounced his judgement, incurable cancer." She just laughed. Then she asked Jayaprakash to arrange a get-together at the Indian Express Guest House. Many friends and colleagues came to meet Prabhavati, held her hands and wished her good luck. With a mischievous smile she said to them, "Behind your good wishes is a poignant good-bye." She passed away soon after the get-together at the Indian Express guesthouse. JP after his wife's death said, "I have lost all interest in public life and politics. I do not see any new people's power emerging. But then in Bihar and Gujarat I have found the new wave of anti-corruption movements. I see a ray of light; a new power emerging in the youth."

Youth Power

JP started talking about Total Revolution in which youth should play a great role. He proposed that the revolution should be multi-dimensional, encompassing the political, social, economic, moral aspects of Indian society. His sensitivity to people's miseries brought him back to active politics in 1974 to lead the emerging youth power. Initially he mobilized youth power to fight against corruption and subversion of democracy in Bihar and Gujarat. During this period JP wrote, "I am groping in darkness, but I see a new rising force of youth power at this old age." On 4 November 1974, JP led a huge procession in Patna, which faced teargas and lathi-charge. The army was called in to control the public outburst. At one stage a jawan hit JP with his baton, and JP fell down. This moment was captured by the photojournalists present at the occasion and was widely published in the newspapers the next day. JP and his colleagues had demanded the dissolution of the Bihar Legislative Assembly. Some political pundits questioned the legal sanctity of demanding the dissolution of a democratically elected Assembly.

JP defended the demand for the dissolution of Bihar Legislative Assembly on the basis of the view expressed by A.G. Noorani, an eminent lawyer from Mumbai. JP had great respect for A.G. Noorani for his legal acumen and intellectual abilities. At various meetings of intellectuals as well as activists, Noorani had quoted a relevant extract from the book, *'Law of Constitution'* by Diecy, a Jurist of international repute, who had observed, "Dissolution of Parliament is an appeal from the legal to the political sovereign". JP often told youngsters, "Here is the legal justification of our demand for dissolution of Bihar assembly".

In the meanwhile, Morarji Desai went on a fast unto death demanding elections to the Gujarat assembly. He demanded, " Either election will take place or I will die." I remember Indira Gandhi's response to Morarjibhai's fast. I was in the Lok Sabha when Indira Gandhi, in her characteristic style declared," We cannot be pressurized like that and we shall not yield and we shall not promise elections in Gujarat. "The fast continued and continued to galvanize the public opinion against the corrupt regime in Gujarat.

One day she came running to the House and said, "Mr. Speaker, Sir, I want to make a statement. We do not want a patriot like Morarji Desai to die and we announce that elections will be held and the schedule will be announced at a later date." When she made this announcement, I got up and said, "Mr. Speaker, Sir, she had repeatedly said, 'no, no, I won't accept this demand', but when a lady says, 'no' again and again, somewhere in the heart of hearts, it means 'yes'." This comment sent the House into a roar of laughter. Indira joined others as well and laughed heartily. This event in my view was a new phase in the battle against corruption and battle for democracy. Then JP said, "The turn of events has given me a new light. The power of youth has to be mobilized all over the country." JP began to travel. His message began to resonate all over the country. The youth movement became very powerful during that time.

12

1975-77: Emergency

JP Movement in Bihar

JP called me to Patna along with some leaders of the CPI (M). It was decided that we would draft a statement extending our support to the JP movement. A long statement was prepared. JP saw that and said humorously, "In my old days I used to write in this language... Madhu knows my style, let him prepare a draft and I will see if any change is necessary." For me, it was a matter of pride and I prepared a brief statement reflecting the style of JP and showed it to him. He approved the draft. He said, "Done. This statement will go in the name of everyone present here." The statement was published by CPI (M) in their journal. The statement spoke about the issues of the people, the working class, the peasantry and the poor. The movement then became broad-based; the CPI(M)'s support gave a new impetus to the movement. This new situation stirred the people and on the other hand it also hardened the attitude of Indira Gandhi towards the political parties opposing her policies. Elections were held in Gujarat and a new Government, headed by Babubhai Jashbhai Patel, was installed. The government was called Janata Sarkar (government). In Bihar a widespread movement gained momentum. A large number of legislators resigned. It became very clear that JP's call for Total Revolution would soon spread all over the country. The spark, in Bihar and

Gujarat, was poised to ignite the whole country. At that time some radicals even questioned whether an anti-corruption movement could bring about a revolution in India. Acharya Kripalani commented, "Look at the changes that had taken place in different parts of the world. In France corruption brought about revolution. In Chiang Kai-shek's regime in China, it was corruption that brought about revolution. In Syngman Rhee's regime in Korea again, it was corruption, which brought about revolution. Corruption is also a very major bane, which hits the poor the most." Corruption became the focal issue of JP's movement. The anti-corruption movement turned into the movement for the preservation of democracy in India.

Indira Gandhi used the electronic media in a manner typical of totalitarian regimes from around the world. The Indo-Soviet Pact had been signed on 9 August 1971. I.K. Gujral was the Minister in charge of Information and Broadcasting and Sanjay Gandhi contacted him and said, "We have to organize a huge youth rally, to counter JP's movement and it must be telecast live." At that time Sanjay Gandhi was the leader of the Youth Congress. Gujral said, "I won't take instructions from you; you have nothing to do with government and you have nothing to do with the Ministry of Information and Broadcasting." Indira Gandhi was annoyed with Gujral, for not following the instructions from her son, and he was relieved of the Information and Broadcasting portfolio.

The JP movement went on gaining strength. I remember that after JP retired from politics (in 1954), whenever he came to stay at the Mani Bhawan in Bombay, where Mahatma Gandhi used to stay, meetings were organized and people were informed about JP's visit. About 50 to 100 people would come to meet him. But during the movement of the 1970s, lakhs of people came to listen to JP from all over the country. It was obvious that he received a far greater response from the masses during the 1970s than he did ever before.

Call for Army's Revolt

Politicians have the tendency to twist issues when they are in power. Anticipating that the government might try to suppress the movement through army or police intervention, JP made a public appeal, "I want the army and policemen to defend the tri-colour and India. That is your major responsibility. If anybody asks you to destroy the democratic content of life and attack people, I would like you to apply your own judgment." It was not at all a call for revolt by the Army and the police. However, within and outside India a campaign was carried on that JP was provoking a revolt in the Army and the Police. He was attacking corruption at that time and the ruling party was the target of that attack. There were people who carried on a campaign that JP was almost asking people to revolt and take up arms, and ask the army to revolt. JP said, "I am not asking our forces to revolt. I have only said that the soldiers are not expected to accept illegal orders."

Later, during the Emergency, when I was in Bangalore jail, I studied all the documents related to this controversy. When I was released, I also extended my full support to JP's call for the defiance of illegal orders. In defence of my position on this issue, I would provide precedence from the judgments in the American courts. The U.S. courts have repeatedly held that an American citizen has the right to ignore not only an executive order, if he considers it illegal, but even a law if he thinks it is unconstitutional. As far as U.S. servicemen are concerned, the Articles 90 to 92 of the Uniform Code of Military Justice (UCMJ) provide elaborate guidelines for punitive actions. Specifically, in the explanation of the term, 'lawful action', the Article 92, (Failure to obey order or regulation) says, "A general order or regulation is lawful unless it is contrary to the Constitution, the laws of the United States, or lawful superior orders or for some other reason is beyond the authority of the official issuing it." This explanation gives the U.S. armymen the absolute right to disobey any unlawful order of a superior officer.

At the Nuremberg Trials many Nazi officials had pleaded that they were only executing orders while perpetrating crimes against humanity for which they had been charged. This plea was not regarded as a valid defence. The Charter governing the decision of the Nuremberg Tribunal was later on referred to the General Assembly of the United Nations, which affirmed the principles recognized by the Charter and asked the International Law

Commission to reformulate them. The Commission did so and codified them in the shape of seven principles and one of them is, 'A person who commits an act, which is a crime under International Law, cannot be absolved from the liability because he is carrying out orders of his government or his superiors.'

In response to the allegations hurled at JP, I cited the above references in my articles and speeches and repeated them in Parliament as well. The Congress members kept quiet when I produced these precedents. I quoted the chapter and verse of what was accepted in International Law: " Those who have committed crimes against humanity cannot be absolved of their guilt on the ground that they did it strictly following the orders given from the top". In fact, at the Nuremberg Trials, this was the core issue discussed. The defenders of the Emergency had the temerity to describe JP as a man who tried to provoke the Army and the Police to defy the orders. To put things in perspective, JP's appeal was to defend the National Flag, India's Constitution and India's integrity. He merely pointed out that if any illegal order was given, there was no obligation on the part of the citizens of the armed forces to obey it. Subsequent turn of events (imposition of Emergency and suspension of civil liberties) vindicate JP's concern that Indira Gandhi was toying with non-democratic actions.

JP rose to great heights of popularity during that movement. Indira Gandhi was nervous and frustrated by the turn of events. She had lost the elections in Gujarat, the legislators in the Bihar assembly had revolted, and JP was attracting lakhs of people throughout the country. Her restlessness was aggravated when it was reported to her that at the Ramlila grounds JP had provoked the army and the police to revolt. Indira ordered the arrest of JP. Immediately after his arrest Indira declared a State of Emergency and suspended the civil rights of all citizens. Imposition of Emergency was executed in an illegal manner.

The Indian Constitution has given the right to declare a state of Emergency only to the Cabinet, which alone has the power to make the recommendation for declaration of Emergency to the President. Without involving the cabinet, Indira Gandhi sent the documents recommending imposition of Emergency to the President

Fakhruddin Ali Ahmed. It was only the day after, that she convened the Cabinet and completed the formality of Cabinet endorsement of the document she had already forwarded to the President as a cabinet decision. Sending the ordinance to the President the night before its consideration by the Cabinet was a total violation of constitutional requirements and an illegal act.

I would like to repeat that the movement for Total Revolution provided JP with a new purpose in life. After the death of Prabhavati, he was dejected, but he recognized the spark in the youth power in Gujarat and Bihar. He helped turn that spark into a torch, which he carried throughout the country. I think JP's call for Total Revolution and his relentless campaign around the country rejuvenated the nation.

Promulgation of Emergency

I do remember a cartoon of Abu Abraham, which vividly portrayed the way the President, was treated. The cartoon depicted the President sticking his hand out of the bathroom through a small opening in the door to sign the ordinance proclaiming the state of Emergency. The cartoon showed the President saying, "If there are any more, then please wait; I will sign them, as soon as I get out."

Emergency Challenged in Court

Those of us, who were detained in the Bangalore Central Jail, during the Emergency, decided that we should carry on our fight from the jail. We decided to use the time available to study the legal provisions and present our viewpoint before the judiciary. After careful study of various legal aspects of the Emergency conditions, we filed a Habeas Corpus petition. The petition was divided into two parts. The first was Habeas Corpus against our detention and the second part of the petition challenged the legality of the promulgation of the Emergency. The judge who heard our case asked whether we had anything to say regarding this petition. We said that we would like to see that this case be disposed off as early as possible so that we would be able to go back to Parliament to continue our work, because those of us who were the petitioners like Atal Bihari Vajpayee, Lal Krishna Advani, Shyam Nandan Mishra and myself were all Members of Parliament. The judge provided a very good response. He said, "In England if a Habeas Corpus petition comes up before the court, it is disposed off within a day or two. The civil liberties of a citizen are very important in a democracy." The case was transferred to another judge in Bangalore. The new judge gave us additional time for preparation of our arguments. It is indeed surprising that on the morning of the hearing at about 7 a.m., we received a release order. Meanwhile Atal Bihari Vajpayee was released on parole, as he was not feeling well. The police told us to pack up and leave the jail. As soon as we came out of the jail, we were handed over a Central Government warrant of arrest and then taken by plane to Delhi. We reached Delhi at midnight. As we were herded into a truck, Shyam Nandan Mishra said, "We are not criminals; we are MISA (Maintenance of Internal Security Act) detainees." The policeman said, "I do not care who you are. You just sit here in the truck." And after sometime we found ourselves in Haryana at the Rohtak Jail entrance.

"Search Your Soul"

I must narrate details of a comic situation that helped relieve the tension of this entire episode. When we came down to the Rohtak Jail, the Deputy Superintendent conducted a body search on each one of us. Those being searched included Lal Krishna Advani, Shyam Nandan Mishra and I. Shyam Nandan Mishra was wearing plastic footwear. The policeman took the footwear away from him and tore open its sole to see whether any documents were hidden inside. Shyam Nandan Mishra was very annoyed. In Hindi, he said, *"Yeh kya badtamiji kar rahe ho? Meri chappal tod rahe ho!"* (What are you doing? You are tearing off my footwear!!) I tried to calm the situation with a humorous comment. Just two days earlier the newspapers had reported a statement of the Prime Minister Indira Gandhi that the Opposition must search its soul. Citing this statement, I told the Deputy Superintendent of Jails, " The Prime Minister has asked us to search our souls. She meant 'soul', not the sole of our footwear." Everyone including the Deputy Superintendent of Jails and Shyambabu started laughing.

Shyambabu was asked to go ahead. At the Rohtak Jail we had the company of Piloo Mody, Biju Patnaik, Sikander Bakht, Ram Dhan and many other important leaders who were already detained at the Rohtak Jail when we were brought there.

Habeas Corpus Petition

The judge at the Bangalore High Court, where we were supposed to appear, made it clear to the government that in first releasing and then re-arresting us, the government had not acted correctly. From the Rohtak Jail we had already sent a message to the judge that we wanted to appear before the Bangalore High Court. In response to our application, he gave a ruling that we should be produced before the court on a particular day. He gave the government one month's time. He said, "I am not dismissing the case forthwith. But I am giving you one month's time. After that period the petitioners should be brought to my court". The government opposed the judge's order and put forward an argument that "from the security point of view bringing these leaders to Bangalore was not feasible." The judge insisted, "No, they are not criminals and there is no threat to their security; they should be brought back." So again, when the case began, we were brought back to Bangalore. We were very happy that top ranking men of the legal fraternity pleaded our case. For instance, the first to rise on our behalf was former Chief Justice M.C. Chagla. I remember the judge told him, "Mr. Chagla, You are very old. You can take your seat and argue." Mr. Chagla said, "No Sir, today I might tell you that it is my birthday; my family members were keen that I should remain at home to celebrate my birthday. The freedom and liberty of citizens is more important than my birthday. However, I have come here to defend democracy and I can argue the case of these detainees while I am standing. Even if I collapse while defending the liberty of the people, I think, I would not mind it at all." He argued the case cogently while standing throughout the proceedings. Shanti Bhushan also came to defend us. D.M. Chandrashekhar was the judge".

The government meanwhile decided to go to the Supreme Court challenging the right of the MISA detainees to challenge the MISA order. So, when we were brought back to Rohtak, we found that the Supreme Court had struck down our right to challenge the MISA order. As a result of the Supreme court ruling, the judge said, "Since the Supreme Court has already dismissed the writ petition challenging the MISA and has declared that detainees under the MISA have no right to challenge the Emergency and to challenge their detention, we have struck down this petition, as the decisions of the Supreme Court over-rides all other decisions." The judge formally asked each one of us, "Have you any statement to make?" I got up and made an oral statement, "When we were detained under the MISA, as a last resort we came to you in the court for the defence of our freedom and liberty. Now the Supreme Court decision has come and, therefore, you have no alternative but to dismiss our case". The government did not like some of the interim orders issued by the judge during the trial and censorship was imposed on their publication. We said to the judge, "I know that our liberty is lost. Your Lordship, long live your liberty." Thus the case was dismissed. We came back to the Bangalore Central Jail and then stayed there till we were released. First they released the MPs and then the rest of the political prisoners.

Torture of Detainees

During our stay in Bangalore Central Jail, I sent a letter to the Prime Minister condemning the manner in which two of our colleagues, were treated. First, I referred to Mrinal Gore who went underground when the Emergency was proclaimed and was arrested much later. She was taken to a very old jail at Akola in Maharashtra. She was put in an old barrack, which was not in use for many years. Before her arrival at this prison the room was used like a dumping room. Items in the barrack were stacked in corners and some space was created for her. In the adjacent barrack there was a woman suffering from leprosy. In a barrack opposite Mrinal's was a deranged girl who screamed through the night. Obviously Mrinal was detained under conditions that caused her immense mental torture. I wrote to Indira Gandhi saying that it was most disgraceful and it was an irony that a leading political worker should be treated like this when the world was celebrating the International Year of the Woman.

Another matter I took up with Indira Gandhi concerned Lawrence Fernandes, a brother of George Fernandes. He was detained at the Bangalore Central Prison. The story of his arrest is also interesting. One day early in the morning police from Bangalore came to the residence of Alice Fernandes, mother of George and Lawrence. They said, "We want to take Lawrence Fernandes to the police station for some time and we would send him back." He was taken to the police state on very early in the morning. He did not come home at all. His mother went to the local police station to inquire about his whereabouts. She was told that they were not aware of Lawrence's whereabouts. Then after a week of detention, Lawrence Fernandes was taken to a cell where only those who were guilty of murder were kept, with shackles on his feet. I was in the Library and from behind I could see that it was Lawrence Fernandes. So I shouted, "Oh, is it Lawrence?" He shouted back at the top of his voice, "Yes, Madhu, I am Lawrence. I have been beaten up and tortured and then kept forcibly in a closed cell." In that cell one life-timer was asked to give food to him every day. We persuaded this life prisoner to give a note to Lawrence Fernandes while he took food for him. I had asked him to write down everything about the treatment meted out to him from the day he had been arrested till he came to the prison. He gave all the details to this prisoner who clandestinely passed on the note to me. The note carried the minutest details of the gruesome treatment meted out to him. Lawrence was moved from one police station to another and was beaten up by the aerial roots of the banyan tree till he became unconscious. At one time, when the policemen were deliberating as to what was to be done, one of them felt that he was already dead and said, "Sir, should we go and throw his body on the railway lines. People will think that he died while crossing the railway lines and there will be no inquiry." They were speaking in Kannada, not realizing that Lawrence Fernandes' mother tongue was Kannada as well. We managed to send this information out.

Letters to PM

I will not disclose the name of one Congressman who used to visit us occasionally. I gave him the letter. Once earlier when I sent a letter to the Speaker with an enclosed letter for Indira Gandhi, the Speaker had said, "You send it directly to her." So in this instance, when the Congressman came to the jail for some work, I contacted him through the Jailor and told him that I was enclosing a letter addressed to the Prime Minister Indira Gandhi, and that he should give it to Ramakrishnan who was my Secretary with the instruction to put it in the Lok Sabha box. I knew that when a Member of Parliament puts a letter in the Lok Sabha box in the name of the Prime Minister, nobody would open it. It goes straight to the Prime Minister. This letter was written on 14 January 1976. In this letter I wrote:

> *Madam Prime Minister,*
>
> *It was hard to reach you, but now this letter will be right on your table because it has gone through the Lok Sabha box.*
>
> *After six months of my detention, I am addressing this letter to you not to ventilate any personal grievance of mine, but to bring to your notice the most disgraceful treatment given by the government to my colleagues. Mrs. Mrinal Gore, a Socialist MLA from Bombay city was arrested at Bombay on December 21, 1975, and was detained under the MISA at Bombay Central Prison on the basis of order of June 26, 1975. She was then served with another order of the Government of Maharashtra on December 25, 1975 and on the basis of this order she was removed to the remote Akola Central District Prison in the Vidharba region of Maharashtra, so as to isolate her completely from all other political detainees. For last 100 years, the Akola District Prison has not accommodated any female political detainee. Mrs. Mrinal Gore has been done the singular honour to be in this prison.*
>
> *It is of significance to note that almost all the political detainees from Bombay city have been kept either at Yeravda or at Nasik Central Prison. Mrs. Mrinal Gore was put in a barrack, which had one door, but no window at all. A female*

criminal in an advanced stage of leprosy was put in the adjoining cell and Mrs. Gore was made to use the same latrine as was used by the leper. Just opposite to Mrs. Gore's barrack at a distance of 20 feet was lodged another female prisoner who is a violent lunatic. This prisoner wears no clothes and stinks awfully because of her failure to take bath for months and indulges in shrill shrieking day and night. Obviously Mrs. Mrinal Gore was lodged in the Akola District Prison under the inhuman conditions only to cause her mental and physical torture. The disgraceful treatment given to her is the most ugly expression of the Government's callous and vindictive attitude. It is a matter of shame that after celebrating the International Women's Year with such fanfare, selfless and dedicated political worker and vigilant legislator like Mrs. Mrinal Gore should have received such an inhuman and uncivilised treatment at the hands of the Government. I fully realise that you will not care even to acknowledge this letter when you have chosen not to reply to the communications from a person of the stature of Shri JP who today symbolise the conscience of the Nation. I have addressed this letter only to put the records straight and to give expression to my indignation over the ugly treatment meted out to my colleague Mrs. Mrinal Gore. What else can a detainee do from behind the prison bars? I am quite conscious of the consequences of this letter. I can well imagine that through this communication, I am likely to incur your wrath and get my detention prolonged. However, I feel least worried about it. I will remain completely undeterred even if the prison yard from which I write this letter were to become my graveyard.

Rest assured that in this land of Mahatma Gandhi, my will to fight for freedom will ever remain more powerful than the engine of repression that seeks to suppress it.

Yours sincerely,

(Madhu Dandavate)

I wrote another letter on 22 May 1976 after getting more details from Lawrence:

> *Bangalore,*
> *May 22, 1976*
> *Madam Prime Minister,*
> *In a mood of anguish as well as indignation, I am addressing this letter to you. I was shocked and pained to find that Shri Lawrence Fernandes, the brother of Shri George Fernandes was brought to the Bangalore Central Prison on 20 May in a completely shattered condition and was taken straight to a prison cell in a police jeep. As Shri Lawrence Fernandes was brought down from the jeep, he was limping and had to be assisted by the police to take him to the cell. He was taken into the police custody at Bangalore on 1 May 1976. And during his confinement in the police lock-up for twenty days, he was brutally tortured with the sole purpose of extracting information regarding the whereabouts of his brother, Shri George Fernandes. Not to leave any visible mark of torture on his body, Shri Lawrence Fernandes was taken to three doctors on three different occasions. Every time his real identity was concealed and he was taken to the doctor under some fictitious name of a police officer. The physical torture was so severe that at one stage the police as well as Shri Lawrence Fernandes feared that he might die. During this torture, the police threatened that if Shri Lawrence Fernandes refused to give information about his brother, Shri George Fernandes, he would be thrown on the railway track leaving no trace of their action.*
>
> *They also warned him that if he reveals the details of torture either to the Magistrate or to others, he would have to face dire consequences. Obviously to make the visible marks of torture less conspicuous, Shri Fernandes was kept in the police custody from May 1st to 20th. Though he was taken into police custody at Bangalore on 1 May, he was produced before the Magistrate at Devangere about 180 miles away from Bangalore on 10 May 1976. Shri Brahmanand Reddy, the Union Home Minister, had made a statement on the Floor*

of Lok Sabha, that the police were instructed not to misuse their powers and had assured to give human treatment to the persons arrested. The physical torture of Lawrence Fernandes makes a mockery of this assurance. The detainees and other political prisoners in the Bangalore Central Prison are observing a fast today to protest against torture of Shri Lawrence Fernandes. The echoes of this torture will he heard in legislature. The deaf ears of tyrannical government may not hear their voice, but the protest is intended to stir the consciousness of the people. Rest assured that people's wrath against all such atrocities will one day find utterance and people will settle the account of all that has happened.

Yours sincerely,

(Madhu Dandavate)

Some friends in the Bangalore prison did not want me to send this letter. After receiving the letter Indira Gandhi contacted the Home Ministry in Karnataka. She asked her Home Secretary to find out how I could get all these details when I was in detention. She also asked for the details of what happened to Mrinal Gore and Lawrence. She feared that the news had leaked out because the political prisoners were allowed to move freely within the jail premises. We were allowed to walk around in the prison garden and visit the Library. As a result of my letter to Indira Gandhi the door of the barracks, in which we were kept, were locked up and we were not allowed to move out of the barracks any more.

As far as I remember we were locked up in October and not allowed out for ten months until August 15 the next year.

Attitude of Jail officials

We were Members of Parliament at that time. The attitude of Jail officials was not very bad. They did not beat or torture us. I was detained in Bangalore prison with Ramakrishna Hegde and J.H. Patel, both of whom later on became the Chief Ministers of Karnataka, Atal Bihari Vajpayee and Deve Gowda, both of whom later became Prime Ministers, Shyam Nandan Mishra, who later on became a Minister in the Union cabinet, Lal Krishna Advani (later Deputy Prime Minister), and Dr. Jeevraj Alva (under whose Chairmanship a committee was appointed to find whether JP was tortured in Chandigarh or not). With people of this stature as prisoners, they could not do anything brutal. They censored all our letters.

Kidney offered to JP

One day we received the news that JP was very serious. He had kidney trouble. He was on dialysis. I was very disturbed. So I wrote a letter addressed to JP:

> *My dear Jayaprakashji,*
>
> *All of us in the prison here are anxiously waiting for the speedy recovery of your health and normalisation of the functioning of your kidney. One feels like speaking with you a lot through this letter but that will only prevent this letter from reaching you and therefore I refrain from doing so.*
>
> *Through this letter I wish to convey to you my sincere desire that if doctors find it useful from the point of view of your health, I may be operated upon to transplant one of my kidneys to you so that you can live long to guide us all. From behind the bars, this is all that I can offer to restore your health to normalcy. The doctors concerned may be informed of my offer.*
>
> *With regards,*
>
> *Yours affectionately,*
>
> *(Madhu Dandavate)*

JP immediately replied to me. The tragic part of it was that I came to know about this letter only after the death of JP. Our friends from the *Janata* Weekly had kept all the correspondence and after his death they published my letter to him and his reply to me. Then I came to know that he had already replied. He wrote:

Dear Dandavate,

It was a pleasure to receive your letter. I was deeply touched by the offer of one of your kidneys. There are no words in which I can adequately express my feelings, so I shall content myself by saying that I shall remain eternally grateful for your offer, love and the spirit of sacrifice.

My health continues to be poor and it seems that kidneys will take quite some time to recover, if they do at all. In case they do not, I shall have to depend on artificial kidney, as is being done now, which will obviously limit my efficiency and utility.

Now it is over a month and half since I was finally released, but I am keeping myself completely aloof from the movement because I am unable personally to face the consequences of my advice. So I am devoting all my attention to my health. I shall conclude by saying nothing on the present situation to discourage you.

Yours sincerely,

(Jayaprakash Narayan)

Letters to 'family' members

Generally we were allowed to send letters only to our relatives. I had given them a list of about 120 persons; all of them were not my relatives, though a good number of them were. I wrote a letter to Prem Bhasin. "Thank God, your wife happens to be related to my wife, so it is on that ground that I can write a letter to you." When they suspected that I was clandestinely sending letters to people, the intelligence men contacted all the persons whom I was sending letters to. They went even to my son and asked him if he was my son. Then he showed them our correspondence. The intelligence officers also went to my brother-in-law's house.

My wife, one of my younger brothers who was a trade unionist, and I were in detention. At that time my son was very young, studying in the National Institute of Design at Ahmedabad. They did not touch my other relatives.

One day the jailor came and told me, "We have instructions from outside that out of these 120 only 100 are your genuine relations and you can write only to them, not to others."

Damage to JP's Kidneys

JP never had kidney trouble earlier. He was detained in Chandigarh during the Emergency. M.G. Devasahayam, Inspector General of Prisons, has given a detailed description of how he thinks JP might have developed kidney trouble. He has written a full story of the ill-treatment to JP during his detention under the caption 'Prisoner JP in Chandigarh'. He wrote:

The directive from 'Delhi Durbar' was that on 'depositing' JP in the PGI Guest House, I should report to Shri Bansi Lal, the then Chief Minister of Haryana and a key-member of the ruling Emergency coterie. When I called him up, his instructions were terse,

"Yeh sala apne aapko hero samajhta hai!! Usko wahin pade rahne do. Kisi se milne ya telephone karne nahin dena. Aap hi khatam ho jaayega." (This damn fellow thinks he is a hero. Let him lie there. Don't allow him to meet anybody or telephone anyone. He will be finished this way.). Under instructions from the Delhi Durbar and Chandigarh administration I was preparing a contingency plan in the event of JP's death in detention and the death drill was being rehearsed. I was party to this bizarre event of discussing and rehearsing a living man's funeral and it did leave a scar in my mind." The main point at issue was the army's role in such an eventuality and there was strong difference of opinion on this. Former Inspector General of Prisons, Chandigarh, who was in charge of JP, afterwards wrote an article in The Tribune. There he said, "I talked to the doctors and after knowing what treatment they were giving, I was really surprised how JP's kidney trouble developed and when JP himself had said that he never had this problem. There was a very strong suspicion that some medicine might have affected his kidneys.

The first symptoms of some major ailment appeared on September 26, just a day after commencement of preliminary efforts towards reconciliation following JP's letter to Sheikh Abdullah. When asked about this, the doctor said that they are looking into it. For about a month JP was OK, but on October 24, the ailment was back, Severe stomach pain and sweating re-appeared with intensity and was noticed by me when I visited him in the morning. The doctors had no explanation for this. This was again inexplicable and had happened just two days after the delivery of a sealed letter from Lord Fenner Brockway, an eminent British Labour MP, member of Cripps Mission and a friend of India, to JP for which he was contemplating an appropriate and positive response.

The content of the letter was supposed to have been read only by the Prime Minister and came with instruction that even I should not open it. As per directions of the Union Home Minister I had personally delivered this letter to JP unopened. JP opened it, read out and with a smiling face gave it to me insisting that I should read it.

The content of that letter was virtually an apology on behalf of Indira Gandhi for imposing the Emergency and seeking JP's cooperation in restoring normalcy in the country. Obviously, the Prime Minister was keen to end the Emergency at the earliest but there were powerful forces working against it.

Looking back, I feel that ten days, from November 7th to 16th 1975, greatly influenced India's post-Independence history. On November 7, I requested JP's brother Rajeshwar Prasad to write a suitable letter to the PM apprising her of the seriousness of matter. JP's health was deteriorating fast and my suspicion was getting confirmed due to the doctor's hedging replies about JP's health and the disappearance of Lord Fenner Brockway's letter, which was key to the revival of the reconciliation process. Added to this was the intriguing phenomenon of Sugatha (PM's envoy) returning JP's letter to Sheikh Abdullah undelivered.

Under the circumstances, I was convinced that it would be unsafe to keep JP in Chandigarh any longer and he should be sent to a place where his ailment could be diagnosed correctly and treated properly.

This conviction led me to initiate silent and swift steps to launch a multi-pronged assault through the PM's envoy Sugatha, JP's brother Rajeshwar Prasad, Chandigarh Chief Commissioner, Union Home Secretary (Official) and personal channel, on the PMO with the same message content — "If JP dies" — to create a crisis mindset and situation in Delhi. This worked admirably resulting in a flurry of activities leading to JP's release under dramatic circumstances on 12 November 1975 by an order served on him by the Chief Secretary and District Magistrate of Delhi who flew into Chandigarh by a special BSF aircraft.

Talk with JP

JP repeatedly said, "I do not know, I never had this trouble at all. Very strange thing; I never suspected that I would get this disease; I do not know how it came; I do not think that my trouble has developed in the natural course". The reference was to the kidney trouble he had developed in prison.

We were released one by one. Another controversy arose. At that time the parties had not merged and the Janata Party was not formed yet. The Socialist Party was still there. George Fernandes, who was then the President of the Socialist Party, had sent a letter to the National Executive expressing his view that we should not participate in these elections announced by Indira Gandhi. He feared that the elections would be a farce. He expressed the concern that we had very little time to organize or raise funds, and Indira Gandhi would manage the election and emerge victorious. I subscribed to another view in the party that the situation would bring spectacular results for a united opposition. Others holding this view believed that funds would be no problem. People would come forward with contributions. I carried a draft statement to George Fernandes.

George was in jail. He was brought to the court in chains. So I went there and took his signature. I told him, "You had advised the Party that we should not participate in the elections, but we all believe that your thinking is not correct, and want you to please sign this statement supporting participation in the elections." The statement made an appeal to the Indian people to defeat the forces behind the Emergency. I pleaded with George that we should fight with all the vigour and defeat the perpetrators of the Emergency. I took his signature at the entrance to the court. Ultimately, we proved to be correct. Even in the heyday of the Congress when Jawaharlal Nehru was in power, the Congress was popular but it could never win hundred per cent seats in Uttar Pradesh, Haryana, Punjab, and Bihar. Against this background the success of the Janata Party could be termed spectacular because we won hundred per cent seats in all these states.

Intelligence of Intelligence Department

I said in my victory rally, "We are thankful to the Intelligence Department for painting a very rosy picture of the situation in the country and the prospects of the Congress coming back to power under Indira Gandhi. That saved us." Our government was formed. Many of us who were in jail became Ministers. I became the Railway Minister.

Supporters of the Emergency claim that because of strict discipline, the general performance of the government had improved. Now, if you take the conditions inside a prison, there is a rigidly enforced discipline. The prisoners do a lot of work in prison. They function with great efficiency, while the guard is standing with a weapon in his hand. We do not call it an augmentation of efficiency. During the Emergency there was an institutional failure, which had a long drawn effect on politics, the economy, and the process of eradicating poverty. To be specific, during the Emergency, the Constitution was mutilated, democratic norms were destroyed and the freedom of press was taken away. As a result, the press was not even allowed to report Parliamentary debates without censorship. When the pros and cons of any issue were discussed in the Parliament, only the government's perspective was allowed to be reported in the media. Administrative and economic failures were kept secret. The level of corruption during the Emergency had gone up, but this information was kept under wraps. Only when the Emergency was over, could it be understood that under the garb of imposed discipline during the Emergency, corruption had in fact increased.

Small Maruti Car

I would give you a specific example of the corrupt practices during the Emergency period. Before the Emergency, the then Industry Minister Fakhruddin Ali Ahmed announced in the Parliament, "The broad policy of the government is not to encourage the expansion of the automobile sector but to encourage manufacturing of those vehicles, which are used by the common people." In violation of this declared policy, Sanjay Gandhi was granted permission to install a plant to manufacture a small Maruti car. When this matter was raised in Parliament in the 5th Lok Sabha, the concerned Minister was threatened that he should not divulge all the facts that would reveal all the improprieties that happened in granting permission to the Maruti project. This matter was again raised in the 6th Lok Sabha and it was proved that the previous Indira government had committed a number of irregularities in granting permission to Sanjay Gandhi.

Many other cases of corruption had taken place during the Emergency simply because the citizen's right to question the rulers was taken away. The bureaucracy was under threat. They were forced to follow instructions from the coterie around the Prime Minister without consideration of legal norms or prescribed policies. This deterioration in the democratic functioning had a long-term impact on the economy. The impact could be gauged from the introductory part of my speech while presenting the Finance Budget for 1990-91.

Let me, at the outset, deal with the economic situation that we inherited from the previous government. I do so not in a spirit of acrimony, but with a view to reveal the ground realities. The Central Government's budgetary deficit was 13,790 crore rupees as on 1 December 1989, a level nearly double the deficit projected for the whole year in the 1989-90 budget. Wholesale prices had risen by 6.6 per cent since the beginning of the financial year. The balance of payments was under strain and foreign exchange reserves excluding gold and SDRs (Special Drawing Rights) were down to an amount of 5,000 crore rupees. Stock of food grains had fallen to 11 million tons. On a broader scale the Economic Survey, which deals with the current economic situation was placed on the Table of the House, only a few days ago. I will not go into the details, but will highlight only a few points.

There has been some slowing down of growth in 1989-90. GDP (Gross Domestic Product) is expected to rise by 4 to 4.5 per cent, industrial output by about 6 per cent and agricultural output by 1 per cent or so on the peak level reached in the previous year.

The price rise this year affects several commodity groups and the pressure of inflation is clearly linked to the fiscal imbalance. The Budget deficit and money supply growth have been running mill about the target. The Revised Estimates for 1989-90, which I will present a little later, indicate that the budget deficit is expected to be substantially higher than Rs.7337 crore rupees projected in the budget estimated for 1989-90. The growth rate of aggregate monetary resource was 16.5 per cent from the beginning of the financial year to 23 February 1990.

As regards the trade performance this years exports have grown at the rate of 38 per cent and imports at 21 per cent in rupee terms in the first nine months of the year. But the pressure on reserves continues, as the improvement on trade account is not sufficient to counter-balance the increase in debt service obligation. I have drawn attention to these features in order to highlight the constraints within which the new government has to look for ways of fulfilling its mandate.

Understand that during the Emergency, critical issues were not even discussed by the cabinet. Only the formality of presenting it to the cabinet was followed. Decisions were pushed through by a coterie and pushed through the bureaucracy. Even if bureaucrats pointed out inadequacies or improprieties, they were taken to task. The notion that the Emergency had some positive impact is incorrect. Some people say that trains were running on schedule during the Emergency. A similar argument was put forward after Mussolini was thrown out of power. The new government was told that during the dictatorship, the trains were running on time. The people in the government answered, "Yes, formerly the trains might have been running on time, but now the trains run in the right direction!"

Poverty, which is at the root of many problems in India, was completely neglected during the Emergency and the scheme to eradicate poverty was not implemented. The peasants were prevented from organising demonstrations to highlight their problem. Industrial unions could not undertake strikes. I do not agree with the concept of imposed discipline during the Emergency because the environment suppressed the voice of those who could ventilate some of the failures of our economy and project their legitimate demands. The fact that the Emergency played havoc with our country's economy came to light when proper economic surveys were carried out after the Janata Government took over. I do not agree with the point of view that during the Emergency, though the freedom might have been lost, bread was protected. Jayaprakashji once said " The difference between Democratic State and the Totalitarian State is that even if bread is not available in a Totalitarian State, the hungry man has no freedom to say, he has no bread". That is actually what was happening during the Emergency. All the agonies and distress were driven below the carpet.

Family Planning discredited

In fact, I have always been worried about the way the population is growing in this country. Not through coercion, but through incentives and disincentives and through a planned programme, the population has to be controlled. I believe that family planning is a programme of national importance. Bad management and the excesses of the Emergency period destroyed the programme. Anyway, though the Emergency period was over, the urgency of that programme was undermined. This was a negative consequence of the post-Emergency political developments.

There are countries where the population is very low, and governments have to give incentives to increase the population. In our country we have already crossed 100 crores. A poor country cannot afford such a large population. But then the minorities had a feeling that forced sterilization would perpetually keep them in a minority. At that time Collectors, ration shopkeepers, everybody was given a quota. In my area one old man was put on the sterilization table. He said, "I am 70, how can I produce a child?" They said, "We are not concerned about your age but we need to meet our quota of sterilization." So, the operations were conducted without consideration to age. It was implemented ruthlessly. Family planning was a good programme, which was destroyed by the atrocities of the Emergency period. The forced sterilization programme revealed the ruthless nature of Sanjay Gandhi. If by chance he were to become a Prime Minister, there would have been a greater problem in the country!

Every section of India was affected by the Emergency. Judiciary, a large number of lawyers, students, women, consumers, minorities, agriculturists and political parties were all antagonized. As a result of that, an upsurge of popular resentment against the Emergency caused the defeat of the Congress party in 1977. I have not seen such a victory in history. Mandela brought victory, but not like the one in India in 1977. In 1977 a number of States responded with a resounding election verdict. Such a volcanic upsurge changed the pattern of the Indian polity. One-party dominant rule was transformed into one-party rule.

As I look back upon my days of detention in the Bangalore Central Prison during the Emergency, I realize that my detention for 18 months afforded me the quietude and the opportunity to write my book *Marx and Gandhi*. It was dedicated to the memory of Shrimati Snehalata Reddy, an eminent artist and my co-detainee in the Bangalore Central Prison. Ailing for a long time and in a serious state of health, she was released only to die as a martyr within a few days thereafter. After the Emergency ended, my book *Marx and Gandhi* was released by Acharya Kripalani, the veteran freedom fighter. The book remains a valuable remembrance of my detention during the Emergency.

13

1977: Victory of Democracy

Prior to the Emergency there was a feeling among the non-Communist Opposition parties that there should be proper unity among the Opposition in order to dislodge the Congress government from the Centre. Many people had brought forward the idea of a Federal Party. I said, "A Federal Party is almost like a Front and Front cannot be a substitute for a political party." My point of view was opposed.

JP clinched the issue

I want to recall how the Janata Party was formed because that is also very important. When the meeting of the important leaders of various parties was held at Morarji Desai's residence, nobody was very keen on giving up the symbols of their parties and to form one party. For two days discussions went on. JP was a man of action. He issued a public statement, "If, after such sacrifices, struggles and detentions, there is no total mobilization of votes against the government that brought the Emergency, there is no chance of the state of Emergency going away." JP's statement had a big impact on the leaders, especially on Morarji Desai. They said, "Yes, we should form a Janata Party." All immediately agreed upon the name. On May 1st, 1977, the Janata Party was formally formed and a decision was announced at a public rally held at the Pragati Maidan in New Delhi. It was decided to adopt the election symbol of Bharatiya Lok Dal headed by Chaudhari Charan Singh, as his symbol best represented the ideology and the core constituencies of all the parties. The new party adopted the symbol of a wheel and inside it a farmer carrying a plough. All the Janata Party candidates fought the 1977 elections on the Bharatiya Lok Dal (BLD) symbol.

I believed that consolidation of opposition forces was inevitable. Historical events supported my belief. I want to point out a similar situation from history. When faced with the danger of Fascism, the leaders of diverse viewpoints, from Stalin to Roosevelt, came together. Some were Communists, others were Capitalists and the rest were Liberal Democrats. They all came together to fight Fascism. If they had not joined hands at that time, Hitler could not have been defeated. I do not want to compare anybody as Hitler within the Indian context. However, the fact remains that the government had assumed dictatorial powers through the declaration of state of Emergency. Excessiveness had taken place around the country and political parties and ordinary citizens lived in a constant state of fear. Without a total mobilization of the non-Congress forces, it would have been difficult to defeat the Congress government, and restore civil liberties.

After achieving the immediate goal of restoration of democracy in India, through a united effort, we were faced with the down side of the unification process. Organizational unity did not result in unity of minds. I do not believe that the ultimate break-up of the Janata Party was caused by ideological reasons alone. Some people have blamed Bharatiya Jana Sangh's insistence on dual membership for the break-up of the Janata Party. It is a fact that, as far as the former Bharatiya Jana Sangh was concerned, it had preserved all its original political organizations intact. The RSS was working as their sister organization and most of the leaders of the erstwhile Jana Sangh in the Janata Party owed their allegiance to RSS. Other leaders from the Janata Party were worried about the power balance in the party. Each constituent of the Janata Party made demands for ministerial portfolios and there were many claimants for the post of Prime Ministership of India. Some leaders wanted Jagjivan Ram to be the Prime Minister; others preferred Charan Singh;

Morarji Desai was also in the picture. Charan Singh feared that if he did not support Morarjibhai then, Jagjivan Ram would emerge as the majority choice for Prime Ministership. He did not want Jagjivan Ram to be the Prime Minister and hence supported Morarjibhai. Ultimately Morarji Desai became the Prime Minister. A committee consisting of JP and Kripalani facilitated the decision through discussions with the newly elected Janata Party MPs.

Differences about Prime Ministership

There was a difference of opinion in the Party. Some members felt that on the basis of administrative experience, Jagjivan Ram would be an appropriate Prime Minister. There were four groups, which had large number of Parliamentarians – Charan Singh's group, the Socialist group, the former Bharatiya Jan Sangh group and the Congress (O) group. Later on we merged and called ourselves the Janata Party.

Charan Singh was against Jagjivan Ram for personal reasons. He said, "I will never allow this man to become the Prime Minister." He had taken a firm attitude. He told many friends that he would accept Morarji Desai but would not support Jagjivan Ram. So, voting did not take place. Then JP and Acharya Kripalani were deputed to take a decision. All parties agreed that Morarji Desai should be the Prime Minister and then the government was formed.

Forty-second Constitution Amendment

During the Emergency, the 42nd Constitution Amendment Bill (this Amendment sought to give immunity from Criminal Prosecution to President, Vice-President, Prime Minister and Speaker of the Lok Sabha in the normal course) did maximum damage to the Constitution. This Amendment had curtailed freedom of the judiciary, freedom of the citizens, etc. So priority had to be given to remove the damage that was done to the structure of the Constitution mainly by the 42nd Constitution Amendment. More than that I feel that the important aspect was, why was this 42nd Constitutional Amendment repealed unanimously? Even when I was in jail and came to know that such amendments were introduced, I was not unduly disturbed. I told my colleagues, "The saving grace for us is Kesavananda Bharti judgment of the Supreme Court which upheld the power of Parliament to amend any part of the Constitution and that judgment drew a fine distinction between amending the Constitution and destroying the basic structure of the Constitution." The rider that was put in the Kesavananda Bharti judgment was, 'While amending the Constitution, Parliament has to see that the basic structure of the Constitution is not disturbed.' The judgment itself made it clear that, "We are not making a full list of what constitutes the basic structure. But only as an illustrative statement, we would say that the secular character of the State, freedom of the judiciary, adult franchise and a few important aspects of the Constitution, which according to the Supreme Court, constitute the basic structure couldn't be touched." The judgment made it clear that the list was not exhaustive, but it was only illustrative. In this background while I was in jail, I assured my colleagues that if the 42nd Constitution Amendment were referred to the full-fledged Constitution Bench, it would not stand judicial scrutiny at all.

We also repealed the Maintenance of Internal Security Act (MISA) soon after we came to power. I think, for the first time after we came to power, the Press was given full freedom to publish the proceedings of the Lok Sabha. Speeches of the members of Parliament such as A.K. Gopalan, N.G. Goray, H.M. Patel, and P.G. Mavalankar, who vehemently opposed the Emergency in their speeches in the Parliament, were not allowed to be published in the press. I had sent a Privilege Notice from the jail indicating that, "Tampering with the proceedings of the House is a breach of privilege of the House." However the privilege issue was disallowed because it was said that the Parliament did not censor the newspapers.

Another major achievement of the Janata government was to remove an atmosphere of fear from the minds of the ordinary people. During Emergency, the family planning programme was implemented in such a manner that it created immense fear even in the remotest corners of rural India. The programme was implemented with coercion and mindlessness. I feel this programme itself was one of the major factors that caused great damage to the prospects of the Congress government in the post Emergency election. Under direct supervision of Congress leadership quotas were assigned to Collectors, and important officers in rural and urban administration were told that they had to ensure that a certain number of operations were performed in order to prevent the proliferation of population. As a result, even old men were subjected to vasectomy operations to boost the statistics. We succeeded in restoring the atmosphere of fear prevalent in the country at that time.

Functioning of Cabinet

I was informed by some of the officers, who were associated with the Cabinet during the previous regime that the agenda of the Cabinet meeting used to be announced and there was hardly any discussion. Cabinet meetings were over in short time. The Prime Minister always controlled all the decisions. This was the situation during the Emergency and even before that. Even if there were some controversial issues, hardly any Cabinet members dared to openly express his or her opinion. So even the Cabinet meetings were reduced to a farce. Against this background, I would like to differentiate the functioning of the Janata Party government from that of the Congress government. When the agenda was circulated, the Prime Minister would take the items one by one. Sometimes he would express his views in the beginning. There was always discussion on every topic. There were moments when the opinion of the majority of the members of the Cabinet was different from that of the Prime Minister. Decisions were made based on consensus of the members after prolonged discussions. During the Janata government another procedure was introduced. Regular informal meetings of the Cabinet were held without agenda. The meetings were held at the residences of different members of the Cabinet by rotation. The host member of the Cabinet was responsible for providing lunch. Informal Cabinet meetings helped set a friendly tone and temper to the functioning of the Cabinet.

An instance that I can provide of the democratic functioning of the Cabinet during the Janata Government days involves my wife.

At one point, milk prices had gone up in Delhi and my wife Pramila, along with a group of poor women, had scheduled a meeting with the Prime Minister. She convinced him that increasing the price of milk was a harsh measure. In the Cabinet, the Prime Minister informally mentioned, "Pramila Dandavate along with a delegation of women met me to discuss the recent price rise in milk." Someone in the Cabinet cryptically said, "It is interesting to have a Cabinet Minister's wife leading demonstrations against the government's policies." I replied, "I am in the Cabinet, not my wife. She has full freedom to take up issues of public importance." Then Morarjibhai said, "Yes, Madhu is right."

A different type of atmosphere prevailed in the Cabinet. Unfortunately, the tensions and pushes and pulls between various groups within the party led to the collapse of the government. JP's comment at the collapse of the Janata government was poignant. He described the event thus: "The garden is destroyed (*Bagh ujad gaya hai)*." But anyway, I think, during its brief period in power, the Janata government restored the much-needed climate of freedom, openness, and fearlessness in the country.

No suppresion of views

I think that there was a change in the functioning of Morarji Desai. His earlier image was that of being very strict, firm and sometimes very dogmatic about his views, and that he was uncompromising in his attitude. However, some of the colleagues who had worked closely with him for a period longer than I had have commented that the Emergency period changed him completely.

I think the disastrous consequences of the Emergency had an impact on each one of us including the Prime Minister.

Impact on Indira Gandhi

The shameful defeat of the Congress Party after the post-Emergency elections and then the supreme Parliament terminating her membership and sending her to jail had its effect on Indira Gandhi. I think the reflections from this experience would have brought her back on the democratic path and deterred her from toying with the drastic measures such as imposing Emergency again.

I feel that she mellowed down. Based on her earlier behaviour, I would have expected her to be revengeful, after returning to power. However, I think her mindset was not the same anymore.

I will give you an example of how the tone of her conversations with the Opposition also changed. When she got elected from Chikmagalur constituency and returned to Parliament, I was the Railway Minister. Normally, all the Cabinet Members remain present when a prominent person takes oath in Parliament, but I was in the Rajya Sabha to give replies to questions related to the Ministry of Railways. When she took oath, I was not present in the Lok Sabha. As I was returning from Rajya Sabha, I was passing by the library and heard her voice behind me. I turned around and said, "Oh, Indiraji, congratulations on your election to Lok Sabha." She returned my compliment with, " Thank you. You have brought distinction to your Cabinet. I am unfortunate that you were not in my Cabinet." I immediately responded, "I was fortunate that I was not in your Cabinet." She took the retort quite sportingly.

While being an ardent opponent of her policies, the artistic side of her personality must be acknowledged. I would like to give you another example of my interaction with Indira Gandhi. After the ceasefire of 1971 Bangladesh war, Indira Gandhi rushed to the House while the House was in debate. She announced, "Mr. Speaker, Sir, I have to make an important announcement. I have come here only to announce that Dhaka has become a free capital of Free Bangladesh." Everyone clapped. And then I got up and said, "Sir, so many people died in carving out the Independent State of Bangladesh, a sovereign State. My heart goes out to the martyrs who died for the cause of Bangladesh and I am reminded about a very old poem, which I had learnt in my school days:

> *Oh, liberty, can man resign thee?*
>
> *Once having felt thy generous flame*
>
> *Can dungeons, bolts or bars confine thee,*
>
> *Or whip thy noble spirit tame?*

I had learnt this poem long ago and I did not remember the name the poet. She got up and told me the name of the poet.

Railway Budget

In 1977 the Prime Minister unexpectedly put the responsibility of the Railway Ministership on me. When I became the Railway Minister, I could not present the full-fledged budget because the budgetary year ends by 31st March, and about the middle of March, our government was set up.

I had to present the first Interim Railway Budget to Parliament within three days of taking over as the Railway Minister. When the Chairman of the Railway Board brought typed sheets to me, I asked, "What is this?" He said, "You have to present the interim Railway Budget after two days. So I have brought the draft." I asked him in a jocular way, "Who is going to present the Budget, You or me?" I added, " I do not read speeches prepared by others. Please give me the data regarding performance, revenue etc. And I will provide the policy thrust. It is anyway the Interim Budget. It is not a full-fledged budget and, therefore, it will not be possible to provide comprehensive policies for the whole year, but some thrust has to be given based on our political commitments."

I had become the Railway Minister in the aftermath of a countrywide Railway Strike. It is important to narrate the events, which led to the strike. The then Railway Minister in the Indira government had invited leaders of all the unions of Railway workers to the Rail Bhawan. Quite a few important union leaders were at Lucknow for the May Day meeting. They were invited to the meeting and taken to jails. Even though there was no call for strike, the response to the arrests was a spontaneous all-India railway strike. I had not seen such a ruthless repression of any other strike. Workers, who had long service and were staying in the government allotted quarters, were thrown out of their houses. There was firing in a number of places and people were killed. Thousands of workers were thrown out of their jobs. I became the Railway Minister immediately after the Railway strike. In my Interim Railway Budget, I began with the process of remedying that injustice. I said, "My first announcement is in the interests of Railways. I would like the illegal action of the government in throwing out thousands of workers out of the job to be reversed." I made an announcement that more than 50,000 railway workers throughout the country, who were still out of their jobs because they had been dismissed, will return to their jobs in the same grade, with the same salary. The railway officers said, "Sir, if you take the strikers back, there will be indiscipline in the Railways. The work culture will slacken and our revenues will plummet. There will be large deficits and you will become unpopular. People will feel that you have not been able to handle the health of the Indian Railways." I said, "I have come to the Rail Bhawan with full understanding of the problems of the Railways. My experience from public life is that if you respond to the legitimate urges of the workers, you can expect reciprocal response from them. You can build an understanding that the legitimate aspirations of the workers will be fulfilled only if they in turn agree to inculcate self-imposed discipline at work and help the Railways generate revenues and improve production." With this belief I maintained that Railways would not suffer as a consequence of my decision to reinstate the workers who were removed from their jobs.

I believed that backward regions remain backward due to poor infrastructure. This situation could be mended by providing better infrastructure for these regions. I gave priority for new railway lines in the backward regions so that infrastructure was made available and the developmental efforts could be speeded.

I worked closely with the unions. They responded favorably to my proposals by offering to work hard to meet the performance target set by me. I also made a direct appeal to the workers as well. Addressing a railway workers' rally I said, "I have brought 50,000 workers back to the work. This is not a simple decision. In the history of the Indian Railways a decision of such magnitude, with such deep impact on the welfare of so many people, has never been made. But in return I also expect your cooperation. Let us generate better revenues for the Railways. I will give you better facilities and better emoluments. But at the same time do not expect that all the revenue generated will be spent only in satisfying the workers. There are needs of developmental activities for underdeveloped regions of our country. Even the passengers and the consumers have their needs. The revenue, which you will be generating, will have to be shared to meet the needs of various segments of our society. I will ensure that you will get a fair share of the revenues you help generate. Let us break this black tradition of continuing deficits of the Indian Railways."

After a few months, I presented the full budget. During my budget speech I said, " For years, the Indian Railway budgets have been deficit budgets. This time, I have not increased the fares, I have not increased the freight rates, but I want the priorities to be changed". The trade unions passed a resolution supporting my proposal for cooperation. The resolution pointedly expressed, "Since such a big decision (about the reinstatement of 50,000 employees) has been taken by the new Railway Minister, at present we will not make any further demands. We will concentrate on fulfilling his expectations and then after producing results, we will put forward our demands." The decision to reinstate the employees removed during the strike had an electrifying effect on the employees. That year was the 125th year of the Indian Railways. I had projected a surplus in my Budget of the order of 85 crore (8.5 million) rupees and the workers worked so hard with this new atmosphere that they gave me 125 crore (12.5 million) rupees of surplus. Often I cited the coincidence in my speeches. I said, "What a remarkable coincidence, the Indian Railways have completed 125 years in operation and we have generated surplus of Rs. 125 crores! Fortunately, the Railway Minister has not grown too old and become 125. Otherwise, it would have been a multiple celebration of the number 125."

The success of Railways received wide acknowledgement, especially from the Prime Minister and the President of India. We had invited the Prime Minister and the President to a public meeting at the venue of the Transport Exhibition Centre of the Railways.

Appreciation from Dignitaries

The occasion was the inauguration of a permanent exhibit of Railway engines and wagons from the past. Prime Minister Morarji Desai (who had the reputation of rarely praising anyone in public) said, "This is one Ministry in which I do not have to interfere. Madhu Dandavate, Minister of Railways, managed the Railway Ministry in a manner that even I would not be able to". In his closing remarks, the President of India said " If I have to recommend a Gold Medal for the work of the best Minister, I would recommend it for Madhu Dandavate". In my concluding remarks I thanked the Prime Minister and the President and said "The credit for the success of Railways does not go to me. I only tried to gauge the pulse of the workers, consumers and the general expectations of the country from the Railways".

I put together a policy framework for protecting the rights of the working class in the Railways. The satisfied workers, irrespective of their political affiliations, often termed the Janata period in Railways as, 'Golden period of the Indian Railways.'

I also decided to bring a just settlement of the workers' demand for bonus, which was pending for a long time. At a public rally at Shivaji Park I had told the railway workers that it would be my endeavour to fulfil their aspirations for bonus. In a way it was a promise. I told the Cabinet, "We have produced a budget of 180 crore rupees and we have actually mopped up surplus of 125 crore rupees. I think in that background we must concede the demand for 8.33 per cent bonus." One of the Cabinet Ministers was hesitant. I made it clear to the Cabinet that I had already assured the workers that their aspirations will be looked after. Another Cabinet member asked me how I could give such an assurance without getting the consent of the Cabinet. I said, "I have not announced the bonus, but revealed my opinion." In response, a very senior Cabinet member said, "You cannot go on making the announcements and then face us with a fait accompli." I expressed my regrets and offered to make amends for publicly airing my views, implying that I would resign. Morarji Desai's Secretary, V. Shankar, passed on a small note to Morarji Desai, which said, "I would suggest that we will think over the Bonus issue later on, but as an appreciation of the fine work that the Railway workers have done and produced a surplus of 125 crore, we will announce 100 crore amenity fund for the workers."

Reforms for People

I knew that corruption at the ticket counter was a big problem. I knew this from my experience as a common man prior to becoming the Railway minister. During the budget I announced that steps would be taken to reduce corruption in Railways. As an experiment I decided that at all the metropolitan cities, we would entrust the responsibility of reservation only to the women employees. Many railway passengers supported my observations about the gender difference in corruption at the reservation counter. This decision was challenged in a few High Courts. Wherever a stay order was given, this practice was stopped. In some states the order was not challenged and hence was put into practice.

I visited railway stations incognito and observed people to familiarize myself with the daunting problems they faced. I found that there was great rush of people on long distance Express trains going to Karnataka, Madras and Kerala. Due to the imbalance in demand and supply of accommodation on these trains, unscrupulous employees within the Railways demanded bribes to provide accommodation on these trains. I was faced with the problem of increasing supply within the constraints of the number of trains our infrastructure could support. I remembered that a number of years ago, when visiting Germany, I had seen double-headed trains. With one engine a train had the capacity to haul 18 or 19 bogies. But trains with two engines are able to haul almost double the number of bogies. I decided to experiment with a new solution of meeting the need for increased capacity. I made a suggestion to the department, "Let us introduce the system of double-headed trains with two engines." The officials' immediate reaction was that it was not possible. They feared that a longer train, when negotiating a curve, would experience jerks and that would create discomfort for the passengers. I said, "Gentleman, unfortunately your Railway Minister happens to be a teacher of Physics and would like to explain why there fears would not come true in the long run." I cited the example of the Bombay double-decker buses. When a driver takes a turn, commonsense tells him that he has to reduce the speed otherwise the bus would topple. Our Physics and

Dynamics tell us that the force to keep it on the track is MV^2/R, where M is the Mass of the body, V is the Speed and R is the Radius of curvature of the path a vehicle is going to travel. Earlier, when the drivers had the experience of driving a single-decker buses only, the mass of the bus was less and the experience of negotiating a curve was based on lower mass. The driver had learned to adjust the speed on a curved road intuitively, though he did not know the equation MV^2/R. When the double-decker buses were introduced in Bombay, the mass of the bus increased and naturally with the new mass, the drivers had to experiment with different speeds. Finally they learned at what speed to turn the bus to avoid jerks.

I also cited the theory of Projectiles in Mathematics. When a mass is thrown in a particular direction, the trajectory and the speed can be calculated using the theory of Trajectory. Being a cricketer, I gave another illustration: On the cricket field, when a player standing near the boundary finds that one of the batsmen is far away from the wicket and wants to throw the ball at the wicket, he knows the angle and speed with which to throw the ball, so it will land exactly at the wicket. This he learns through practice. I emphasised that just like a good fielder on a cricket field, a driver would learn to run the train without jerks. I assured the railway officials that though for the initial two or three months, the passengers of double-engine trains may experience jerks, after the learning period was over the drivers would be able to master the technique and the trains would move as before.

I went ahead and decided to introduce double-headed trains to Kerala, Karnataka and Madras, the destinations where the gap between demand and supply was largest. I allowed two-three months to pass. Then I visited all the three trains on different days and talked to the passengers. I took that officer who was apprehensive about this idea with me. The passengers who travelled regularly on these trains said, "We cannot explain why, initially we experienced jerks but now the ride has been smooth." After our return to the office, I told the Officer, "Did you listen to the passengers? We met a number of passengers and they all gave the same answer. It was a matter of luck that a Professor of Physics became the Railway Minister and so his scientific knowledge was utilised to save a good idea from misplaced apprehension".

New Innovations

Another change that was brought in was introduction of double-decker trains on routes where there was less dust near the lines. Providing extra seats slightly above the existing lower seats almost doubled the capacity of these trains. There was some criticism initially, but things settled later on. The third policy change I wanted to bring into Railways was to cater to the needs of the poor and the middle class. Being a Socialist, I had always seen how poor people, who traveled a lot, especially in long distance trains, travelled like cattle. Those days, the trains had wooden benches. At night, the people would sit or sleep on wooden benches, which were extremely uncomfortable. These benches were sometimes broken. While travelling for conferences in my college days, I have slept on a small shelf like plank at the top, which is meant for keeping small luggage. I wrote to the Department suggesting a scheme of introducing classless trains on select routes. I also suggested that the seating be made with comfortable cushioned berths and backrests. I suggested that drinking water be made available to the passengers by placing *matkas* (earthen pots on wooden stands) on these trains. I wanted to introduce a Lending Library in the train so passengers could borrow books against a deposit. The Department officials were skeptical of these ideas. They said, "Even the ordinary wooden benches are misused and they are broken and we have to spend a lot of money to repair broken wooden benches. If you put the comfortable cushioned benches and cushioned backrest, the passengers will tear them." I replied "In my public life, my experience is that if people demand certain comforts and if you respond and make it available to them, they behave responsibly". The first classless train was flagged off on 26 December 1977. In our discussion on what the train should be named, some officials suggested the name be Eastern Express. I did not like it as much and decided to name it Geetanjali Express since its route was from Bombay to Calcutta, the land of Rabindranath Tagore, the author of the *Geetanjali*. A number of portraits of Rabindranath Tagore were displayed inside the train.

Six months after introducing the Geetanjali Express, I called the officers of the Railway Board and told them, "I am sending a team of university students free of charge on this train. Please give them accommodation at our guesthouse at the destination. I am giving them a questionnaire to do a sample survey in order to know what passengers feel about this train." The report indicated that even after six months had passed, not a single berth or the backrest was torn. Most of the passengers interviewed said, "We were sure that if we tore the cushions or misused the new conveniences, then the administration would cancel this service and again the wooden berths would be back." After the fall of the Janata Government, the next government thought that the new conveniences were an expensive experiment and considered discarding it. But then the authorities said, " Sir, the cushioned compartments have become extremely popular, if you discard this convenience, then we will come under great disrepute. We suggest that it should continue." As a result, all long distance trains now have cushions. I am glad that I was able to make a point that ordinary passengers have a need for the comforts as well.

I want to share another interesting incident. I was travelling from Hyderabad to Bombay by train. I was not a Minister then. While waiting for the Minar Express, (the train that commences from Orissa, where it is called Konark Express and from Hyderabad onwards it becomes the Minar Express) I overheard someone say, "*Arey bhai,* Dandavate Express *abhi tak nahin aai hai*!" So I asked my companion to find out what they were referring to. When my companion enquired as to what this Dandavate Express was, they replied, "Don't you know? Mr. Dandavate introduced this train, when he was the Railway Minister and so we call it the Dandavate Express."

Last Journey

On one occasion, while travelling on a train, a person from the second-class compartment came to see me to convey his good wishes on my 75th birthday. I told him, "After I die, I do not want any memorial. See to it that my body is carried from Delhi to Bombay by train with padded cushions and backrest. It would be a happy and comfortable last journey for me."

My effort during my tenure as a Minister for Railways was also to make Indian Railways safer. I found out that collisions at railway stations were very common. When one train was stationary at a platform and a second train was approaching, the driver would be negligent and ignore the red signal. I also found that there were maximum collisions on the routes from Howrah to Burdwan and Mughalsarai to Gaya. The Research, Design and Standards Organization (RDSO) of the Railways devised a very good system called Automatic Warning System to avoid collisions. The Automatic Warning System sends a signal to the engine driver of an approaching train when the train is approaching the railway station. When this Automatic Warning System was introduced on the Howrah to Burdwan and Mughalsarai to Gaya stretches, the accidents on these routes were almost reduced to zero.

We also tried to convert the unmanned crossings into manned crossings. The decision involved a lot of expenditure. As per the prevailing guidelines, 50 per cent of the cost of manning a crossing was to be borne by the Railways and other 50 per cent by the Municipality or the local administration. Since not many of the Local administrations were willing to incur the cost, I decided that the Railways take full responsibility of converting unmanned crossings into manned crossings in very hazardous locations.

At Perumbur near Madras, the Indian Railways have a production unit, where they produce a certain type of coaches, which are described as anti-telescopic. These coaches provide a foolproof guarantee against damage. I feel proud that I encouraged innovation such as this one, with a view to maximize benefit to the passengers. I enjoyed working with the technologists, engineers, scientists and others who were responsible for innovation within the Railway organization with their efforts, we were able to encourage a spirit of innovation in the Railways. My success as a Railway Minister in our Janata government days is partly due to these people as well. Even today the railway men and the passengers recall our contribution.

Facing Demonstration

I want to share another interesting episode that occurred when I was with the Railways. I was visiting the Administrative Staff College to deliver a speech about the importance of technology in the Railways. As you know, Railway employees have unions that are affiliated to different political parties. As my car was getting close to the college, members of a union, who were carrying tri-colour flags, were standing by the road shouting, 'Madhu Dandavate Go Back', 'Madhu Dandavate Murdabad.' To save me the embarrassment, the pilot of the police car suggested, "Sir, let us not go this way. We should take another way and circumvent this demonstration." I said, "I am a representative of the people and have come from the people's movement. Bring me a step stool." I climbed on the stool and started addressing them. I narrated what I had done in the Railways right from the day I became their Minister. I talked about the bonus issue, about the formula of productivity-linked bonus and how it benefited the workers. The demonstrators started clapping even though their leader kept asking them not to clap, because I belonged to a political party that they were opposing. When I returned from my meeting, the demonstrators who were earlier raising the slogans against changed their slogans to, 'Madhu Dandavate Zindabad (Hail Madhu Dandavate).' Choosing to address them, rather than running away, helped in changing their perceptions.

The All-India Railwaymen's Federation, in view of my past performance, has made me a permanent inaugurator of their annual All-India conference for the past 25 years and more.

Many areas that have scope for improvement still bother me. Theft, for instance, which is largely caused by outsiders who do not belong to the railways. I do not want to blame any one government for this failure. The entire society is faced with the ills of dishonesty, gangsterism and murders. During those days it was not so bad, but even then, I was not satisfied with the results. I do feel that in this area we could have done better.

Railways: Administrative Structure

I am among those who feel that the present practice of drawing the senior management of the Railways from the ranks is good for the efficient functioning of the Railway organization. There is a Chairman of the Railway Board who is assisted by members of the Board, who are assigned portfolios such as staff, engineering, mechanical, electrical, traffic, and finance. Board members generally rise from the ranks. In the government, the civil services candidates are selected on the basis of their performance in the qualifying examinations. They are not required to have specific knowledge of the department they would eventually manage. On the other hand, in the Railways there has been a tradition of assigning the top position in the Board to a person who has lifetime of experience in that aspect of the organization. I do believe that one aspect of the private sector that has to be emulated by the public sector is that there must be professionalism and accountability in the public sector. By drawing upon people with specific skills to manage specific functions of the Railway organization, the Railway Ministry ensures professional expertise at the top level.

14

1979: Betrayal of Mandate

Re-Emergence of Indira Gandhi

Betrayal of the Janata Party helped in the re-emergence of Indira Gandhi. In seeking her support to form a government, Charan Singh took away the legitimacy of the argument against her dictatorial designs and helped fragment the non-Congress vote. After withdrawing support to the Charan Singh government, Indira Gandhi campaigned around the country. She said, "They want to defeat me. Have they got any moral right to defeat me? This man who is coming to you for votes, himself begged for my support in writing to become a Prime Minister. They accuse me of having committed so many sins by clamping the Emergency and that I am the greatest culprit in this country. At the same time they wanted the same culprit to support him." She exposed the contradiction in Charan Singh government's attitude towards her. She travelled and garnered sympathy for her by telling people that she had been treated badly by the Janata government and that the Janata government tried to keep her under unlawful detention. She complained about being sent to jail by the Janata government.

How could she complain about being sent to the jail when she herself put so many of us behind bars during the Emergency? In trying to garner sympathy for herself, she conveniently overlooked the hardships of her political opponents and their families during the Emergency. We were in jail for 18 months. I will give you my own example of deliberate harassment of her political opponents. I was arrested on June 25th 1975 and kept in Bangalore jail and my wife was arrested later and kept at the Yeravada Jail near Pune. Even during the British rule if husband and wife were in the freedom struggle and were detained, they were kept generally in the same jail so that they could have weekly meetings. Some of our friends wrote to Indira Gandhi that we should be detained in the same jail. However, Indira Gandhi refused to respond. When some citizens went to the Court of Law a strange judgement was passed. "Madhu Dandavate would be allowed to go by plane to Pune and see his wife. But he must bear the full expenditure of the air travel, of all the police escorts and also provide 10,000 rupees as a deposit." When I was informed about this judgement, I jocularly said, "What nonsense! Do I have to pay money to see my wife?" In principle, Pramila and I took a decision to decline these conditions. While our friends were willing to collect money for this purpose, we maintained that there were many poor detainees who would not afford to meet under similar conditions. Once we set the precedent, such conditions would have been applied to others also. We did not want to set the precedent. My wife told the Jail Superintendent in a very moving manner, "If both of us survive till the Emergency is lifted, we will meet; otherwise both will independently die in two different jails. There is no question of surrendering to these conditions."

I am often asked if it was necessary to appoint the Shah Commission to look into the excesses of the Emergency. I can only say that there was nothing wrong about it and add very emphatically that the Shah Commission did not in any way bring about collapse of the government.

As far as Indira Gandhi is concerned, some feelers were sent to her by journalists and some political parties that she should express regret in the House for what had happened during the Emergency and admit that these were the aberrations. It was an indirect contact. However, she responded, " If I admit, then some sane members would take a compassionate view and put an end to what had happened, but I feel that others would utilize that confession made on the Floor of the Parliament and will take a very firm attitude." I can understand why Indira Gandhi was hesitating. One incident that must go on record is the discussion that ensued in the party regarding what action needed to be taken against Indira Gandhi. The situation then was not clear on what needed to be done, whether to only admonish her or pass a resolution, demanding regrets or apology from Indira Gandhi. There was a section within the party, which was amenable probably to this and so a General Body meeting of the party in Parliament was held. If I remember right, Ram Jethmalani took a very firm attitude at that General Body meeting of the Janata Parliamentary Party. On the other hand, Raj Narain said, "In this land of Buddha and Gandhi, if the former Prime Minister admits that her actions were undesirable and expresses her apology then we should bury the hatchet." It is interesting to note that in the debate of the Parliament, when Raj Narain was speaking, the members of the ruling Janata Party heckled him saying that the matter should be ended. Charan responded, "There is a lot of substance in what Raj Narain says". The whole atmosphere was such that members of the Janata Party had not forgotten their sufferings of the Emergency period and those feelings ultimately led to the termination of her membership of the House.

During this period, we faced another issue regarding taking up a privilege issue against Indira Gandhi. The question was, "Can this Lok Sabha take up a privilege issue related to the events that occurred during the life of an earlier Lok Sabha?' We had to search for precedents from history. We found one specific event that was relevant to the question we were faced with.

Many years ago, the opposition had introduced a privilege motion against Indira Gandhi for forcing officials to hide information relating to the Maruti car scandal from the Parliament. Newspaper reports had then alleged that when the Prime Minister Indira Gandhi was faced with a series of questions relating to various irregularities in the Maruti car project for discussion in the Parliament, people close to Indira Gandhi threatened the officials of the concerned Ministries. The threat was if they provided any information on the irregularities, they would face dire consequences. In the subsequent Lok Sabha, after Indira Gandhi was defeated the issue was raised in the form of a privilege motion. Then some members objected saying, "What has happened in the earlier Lok Sabha cannot be made a subject matter of privilege in the next Lok Sabha." However, there are precedents in the Parliaments of other democratic countries where there is no bar in taking up issues, which led to violations in earlier Parliaments. The issue about the admissibility of the Privilege Motion related to the Maruti scandal was referred to the Privileges Committee. The Committee came with the report allowing for such an action, with dissenting votes by the Congress Members. It was clearly established that under pressure of the former Prime Minister, the concerned Ministries' officials were threatened. It was considered as the highest breach of privilege of a Parliament and hence the Privileges Committee recommended a very stern attitude. This precedent influenced the decision of the Janata Party government to take a firm stand against Indira Gandhi. The privilege motion was admitted. Indira Gandhi was sentenced and her membership of Lok Sabha was terminated. She went to jail and then a halo of martyrdom was created around her. The debate within the party and in the media moved to the question of what type of action should have been taken. Anyway, in the background of the severe damage done by her to the polity, Constitution and to the people, the public mood was in favour of punishing her. Minorities felt strongly about the forced sterilization programme.

Break-up of the Janata Party

We witnessed a strange spectacle at that time. George Fernandes gave an impassionate speech in Parliament, defending the policies and programmes of Morarji Desai's government. His performance in the Parliament received great applause and received wide publicity. The next day, he decided to leave the party and join Charan Singh under the pressure from his colleagues. This unashamed and sudden turnaround cannot be forgotten for a long time.

I remember my conversation with veteran Congress leader Yeshwantrao Chavan after the No-Confidence Motion, moved by him against Morarji Desai, which led to the collapse of the government. Several times Yeshwantrao said to me, "I thought it would be a ritual; how the hell could we win? You had a brute majority in the House. I could not even imagine that my motion would be carried." But anyway, Charan Singh's men were determined to use the No-Confidence Motion to defeat the government. The government was defeated and then Charan Singh put in his claim for Prime Ministership.

Another irony of the situation was the formation of Charan Singh government immediately after the defeat of Morarji Desai's government. The Janata Party government was formed as a result of a fight against the dictatorial regime of Indira Gandhi and ironically enough Charan Singh formed his government after seeking the support of Indira Gandhi. When she was approached for support, Indira Gandhi demanded a letter from Charan Singh seeking her support. That letter was sent. She was a very shrewd politician. She wanted to document the turn of the events. She relished the fact that Charan Singh, who collaborated with others to defeat her, had to seek her support eventually. Asking for a letter was her way of recording the fact for posterity.

I think Charan Singh was the first Prime Minister who did not occupy the seat of the Prime Minister in Lok Sabha. I remember, that day when we were all sitting in Lok Sabha, and he was to seek confidence of the House. We asked, "Where is he? He has not come." The Speaker got up and said, "He has gone to the President to hand over the resignation letter." As a result, the Lok Sabha was adjourned sine die and we came to know that in the morning. Indira Gandhi had already sent word that the Congress Party had withdrawn the support to the government. The sequence of events lacked respect for democratic conduct and culture from both the sides. Indira Gandhi played her card in such a manner that the turn of events would eventually take away the psychological advantage her opponents had earned from their fight against her dictatorial rule of the Emergency period. As a matured politician Charan Singh should have thought about the repercussions of seeking support from a person and the party against whom he fought during the Emergency. By seeking support of Indira Gandhi, he squandered away the psychological gains of the anti-Emergency struggle. He did not have a clear majority when he agreed to form the government with Indira Gandhi's support. He failed to understand the real motive behind Indira Gandhi's support in his eagerness to become the Prime Minister of India.

I would like to reveal a particular document because I want future generations to remember how betrayals took place in the Rashtrapati Bhawan.

I would like to quote an extract from S.M. Joshi's autobiography (translated from the original Hindi text).

> *After the announcement of Chaudhari Charan Singh's ministry I received an invitation from President Reddy for interview. I was distressed to find that despite the fact that Charan Singh did not enjoy the support of the majority of Parliament members of the Janata Party, Mr. Reddy had invited him to form the ministry. Now what was the sense in my accepting Mr. Reddy's invitation? When Madhu Dandavate's Private Secretary Ramkrishnan gave me the information about invitation from the President, I told him that I would not meet him. Ramkrishnan told me that it would be improper to do so. I, therefore, went to see the President only as a matter of courtesy. After some preliminary talks the President said, 'much depends on what advice you offer to Madhu Dandavate.' I enquired as to what advice I am expected to offer?*

> *President said, that it should be advice as to what should be done by Madhu Dandavate in the prevailing circumstances. I never expected this from the President. I frankly told him that Dandavate wouldn't depend on my advice. He can independently think for himself. And yet I wanted to know what advice should I offer him. The President said, "He should join Charan Singh's Cabinet and accept the Railways portfolio."*

> *I replied, if Dandavate seeks my advice, I would tell him to do exactly the opposite of what you were suggesting. I would advise him never to join Charan Singh's Cabinet. Isn't there something like loyalty to the party? When Morarji Desai's*

*ministry was formed we had taken a pledge to remain loyal
to the party. I will not therefore offer advice to Dandavate, as
you desire. Shall I tell you the truth? I do not think that
Dandavate will act as suggested by you.*

*I did not talk so far about my discussions with the President.
I really felt that it was not proper for the President to make
such a proposal. This was partisan politics in which the
President was indulging.*

*When I returned home I narrated the entire episode to
Madhu Dandavate and his wife Pramila.*

*The conclusion of this episode is that when I think of the
behaviour of those who were put on the high pedestal of power
by the Janata Party, I realize to what extent they had thrown
to winds all democratic principles. Such was the conduct of
the President.*

My reaction was, "I got elected from a coastal constituency and
it is the culture of a coastal area that when the ship sinks, the captain
of the ship sinks with the ship and does not run away..." I feel
honoured that S.M. Joshi told the President, "I am sure that
Dandavate will not accept this suggestion from you." I have
considered this a great compliment from a person who I hold as
my lifetime leader in the struggle for freedom and for Socialism. I
was happy that he reposed confidence in me and even without
consulting me, he could communicate my anticipated response to
Rashtrapatiji. I think, there could not have been a better honour
bestowed on me than the response S.M. Joshi gave to the President.

I think that this was the first time that I witnessed Rashtrapati
Bhawan acting in a partisan manner.

No President has ever told any MP so blatantly to change his
Party. The closest we came to a conflict between the President and
the Prime Minister was during the Presidentship of Giani Zail Singh.
So much is said about Giani Zail Singh's conflict with Rajiv
Gandhi. At that time rumours were floating around about the
possibility of the President dismissing the government. Even during
this period Giani Zail Singh did not provoke anyone to defect. In
the old days, in the post-Independence times, the political ethos
was different. Men of towering stature were at the helm and they

were the products of the ethos of the freedom struggle. Dr Rajendra Prasad was a great scholar and a learned man. Dr Radhakrishnan was a scholar of Sanskrit and an eminent exponent of Indian Philosophy. He used his philosophical bent of mind to guide the country. Dr. Zakir Hussain was devoted to scholastic and cultural pursuits. His association with the Jamia Milia, the Aligarh Muslim University and numerous other institutions marked an era of service to the cause of education in this country. His life exemplified erudition, dignity, nobility and humility. Such were the persons holding high offices in the past. Therefore, what happened at the Rashtrapati Bhawan in this particular case, degraded the high traditions of the office held by such illustrious predecessors.

When Morarji Desai stepped down and Babu Jagjivan Ram became the leader of the Janata Parliamentary Party, and lists of supporters were being prepared, news had already reached Rashtrapati Bhawan that the Janata Parliamentary Party, led by Jagjivan Ram, had acquired a majority and some more groups were likely to extend support. As soon as the news leaked out, the President hastened to invite Charan Singh to form the government, even without verifying from Jagjivan Ram, whether he had succeeded in securing support of majority of MPs.

Charan Singh wanted to be number one. So he sent word to Indira Gandhi, "We will break away and form a separate Party; you support us." He collected signatures of support for that.

In retrospect, I must say that the Janata Party was a heterogeneous combination and there were over-ambitious people in the Party. Unfortunately for them, in our Constitution there is provision for only one Prime Minister. Since such a limitation could not fulfil the ambitions of multiple aspirants, the glorious anti-Emergency victory was converted into a defeat. The manipulation at Rashtrapati Bhawan and in other spheres of political life brought about the denigration of politics. When the prospective Prime Minister sought support from the perpetrator of the Emergency, politics reached the depths of degradation.

While we are discussing the fall of the Janata government through defections, I must go on record about some of the earlier developments. My colleague Madhu Limaye had opposed the Bill against defections. He had some genuine grievances. He said, "You must devise more detailed explanations of defection." He drew a fine distinction between dissent and defection. Madhu Limaye argued, "If the Cabinet size is kept only to one-tenth of the membership of Lok Sabha, then there is no room for people seeking defection from the Party for getting Cabinet posts". I went to Morarji Desai and told him that this was the position and that he had mobilized opposition parties, and the government could fall on this issue. So, he said, "Tell the Speaker that I am prepared to refer this Anti-Defection Bill to the Select Committee and let members of the Select Committee propose any changes and we will modify it accordingly." However, Madhu Limaye was unyielding at that time. He said, "There will be no compromise at this stage." The delay in passing the anti-defection law, combined with Charan Singh's role, brought the Janata experiment to the brink of disaster.

Future of the Janata Party

In a mature democracy, when you raise the expectations of the people, and then if they feel betrayed, there is no greater enemy of yours than the electorate. When the Indian electorate found that the members of the Janata party betrayed JP and the pledge we took at Mahatma Gandhi's Samadhi that we would stick on together, was violated, the masses were very disillusioned. Whenever electorate reacts to the betrayal of election promises, the pendulum of popular vote always swings from one end to another. Promises may raise you to great heights, but disillusionment about those promises takes you to hell. That is what happened with us. Then we suffered the phenomenal defeat in the next elections in 1980. Indira Gandhi came back with a bang.

After the fall of the Janata government, the Janata Party suffered a humiliating defeat in the following election.

I will remember that election as the high point of my parliamentary life. When the election results were declared in 1980, I came to know that while Indira Gandhi was surging ahead to power in 1980, in the Lok Sabha elections from my Rajapur Parliamentary constituency, I scored the highest percentage margin of votes throughout the country. I got 74 per cent of the total valid votes polled in the constituency and my opponent got only 26 per cent votes. This was only a personal victory and not a collective success of our party.

This may have been a grand success for me but it also was a colossal failure of those who have been my valued associates. It is not only so in our case, it had happened with others too. Sometimes people distinguish between individuals and their party. I had nursed the constituency and I enjoyed the confidence of the voters. In free India, eight times consecutively we won that constituency – three times Nath Pai won and I won five times. However it was hard to celebrate one's personal victory when the party was defeated.

I remember an interesting event from the history of British parliament. Winston Churchill replaced the weak-kneed Prime Minister, Neville Chamberlain against whom there was an Adjournment Motion and he was defeated. Britain was in dire straits in the Second World War. So the country needed a strong leader. Winston Churchill replaced Chamberlain to become the Prime Minister of the country and the war was won. Churchill was at the zenith of his popularity. The electorate discriminated between the individual and the party. They felt that to win the War they wanted Churchill, but to control the inflation arising out of the War, they preferred a Labour Government. They threw away Churchill's Party with a big margin, but he was personally elected with a large number of votes.

Sanjay Gandhi's Death

It is very difficult to say what impact Sanjay Gandhi's death had on Indira Gandhi. But it is my hunch that she probably took note of the fact that Sanjay went beyond his mandate during the Emergency. I have no evidence but with my political insight I feel that in course of time, Sanjay would have been a threat to her power. I do not know whether she was conscious of that. But I have not the least doubt that after the collapse of her government, Indira Gandhi must have realized that she went too far and did not gauge the support JP had amongst the masses.

Looking at the present political situation wherein communal parties and forces, which were isolated in the past have gained respectability and credibility, a question arises whether on the eve of general elections of 1977, the dissolution of all parties opposed to the Emergency and creating a new instrument of Janata Party was desirable.

However, this question has to be judged by considering the situation that prevailed during the Emergency and at the time of the Lok Sabha elections in 1977. JP could by no stretch of imagination be considered as a sympathizer of communal forces, but he honestly felt that total mobilization of vote against the party that clamped the Emergency was the highest priority. Looking at the results of 1977 elections one finds a lot of substance in JP's advice to all parties. While realizing the main objective of defeating the forces supporting the Emergency, it cannot be denied that communal parties, which were marginalized even in the terms of their electoral strength, gained some ascendancy. Gradually they built their strength on the basis of the credibility they had acquired in the 'Janata Era'.

During the Second World War, Stalin, Churchill and Roosevelt, with their totally different ideological commitments, forged a unity to defeat fascism. In the post-World War era, the Allies shared the loaves and fishes of the victory in war. But their unity was strategically inevitable according to them. A somewhat similar situation existed then. The communal forces gaining respectability in the 'Janata Experiment' grabbed power. The Socialist forces, which had played an important role during the anti-Emergency struggle, suffered most at the hands of the emerging communal forces. The Socialists and other progressive forces have a long way to go to reestablish their lost strength. I am reminded of the famous poem of Robert Frost:

> *The woods are lovely dark and deep*
> *But I have promises to keep*
> *And miles to go before I sleep*
> *And miles to go before I sleep.*

During the euphoria of elections in 2004 communal forces put the leadership of the freedom struggle in the dock with the allegation that the present chaos is their legacy. This is an unkind act. People have totally forgotten the role freedom fighters played under the leadership of Mahatma Gandhi and how Jawaharlal Nehru and his colleagues tried to re-build stability and development on the debris of Partition. We may differ with some of their policies and perspectives but their pioneering work can never be forgotten.

15

Rajiv Gandhi's Succession

The Congress after the assassination of Indira Gandhi

I think, the greatest setback for the opposition was, of course, the unfortunate and deplorable assassination of Indira Gandhi and the emergence of Rajiv Gandhi. The assassination of Indira Gandhi generated a sympathy wave in the country that was more intense than in 1971 (i.e. after the Bangladesh victory). Rajiv Gandhi won the elections riding on this sympathy wave. He played his part to evoke a response to his mother's killing. Obliquely referring to anti-Sikh riots, he said, "When a banyan tree falls, it is no wonder that the earth is shaken." People took the hint. There were widespread riots in the country. The day after Indira Gandhi's assassination, I was travelling by the Rajdhani Express from Bombay to Delhi with my son. There were Sikh families in our compartment. We had to lock the doors of the compartment and bring in the military to save them from attackers. At Tughlakabad railway station I witnessed the cruelest violence against the Sikhs in an organized form. The police did nothing to prevent it. Subsequently the report of the inquiry commission that investigated the anti-Sikh riots has made a special reference to me, for saving lives of several Sikhs on the Rajdhani Express.

When Rajiv Gandhi became the Prime Minister, some people referred to him as 'Mr. Clean'. However it was during his time that the government faced heavy criticism in and outside the Parliament on the issue of purchase of the Bofors gun. I was one of the severest critics of government on the Bofors issue. I had collected all the concerned national and international documents and brought them before the Lok Sabha.

I would like to share an interesting episode. While I was speaking on the Bofors issue, some of my colleagues had jumped into the well of the House and raised slogans. So the Speaker, Balram Jakhar Sahib said, "Professor [he always used to call me Professor] you are making such an eloquent speech, but your colleagues are jumping into the well of the House; you never do it." I said, "No, Sir, I won't do it because I do not know how to swim." In the midst of loud laughter in the House, my colleagues got up and were back in their seats.

Sitting on the Treasury Benches, V.P. Singh made certain revelations and emerged as the spokesman of the Bofors' corruption issue. He told the House, "I have nothing to say. But I won't lie like that." Everybody knew that on this issue he was on our side. When he continued to take this stand, the Congress expelled him from the party. I think V.P. Singh gained political acumen through the anti-corruption stand on the Bofors issue.

The Congress committed a mistake in expelling him. If they had only suspended V.P. Singh then he would have had to follow the Whip of the Leader. Instead he became an unattached member and he had full freedom to put forward his point of view within the House. His integrity was absolutely unimpeachable. Even his opponents never made any allegation of corruption against him. His actions and decisions lent credibility to the anti-Bofors struggle. He was sitting by my side when I concluded my last speech on the Bofors issue with, "Hon. Members of the House, you call Rajiv Gandhi, Mr. Clean, but if anybody can claim to be a Mr. Clean, here he is – Mr. V.P. Singh."

16

Bofors Scandal

I led the Opposition during the entire debate on the Bofors issue. I had delivered four speeches in the course of this controversy.

The scandal concerned the conduct of the government, especially the conduct of the concerned ministers and the Prime Minister in the Parliament. When I initiated a debate on Bofors, the Defence Minister Krishna Chandra Pant made a curt statement, "I wish to make it clear that there were no middlemen involved in this deal and no commission amount was paid at all." The debate continued in the afternoon and the Prime Minister Rajiv Gandhi intervened and said, "I want to repeat what Mr. K.C. Pant has said that there was no middleman and there was no commission that was paid." Then within two days, some additional evidence came in. I made my next speech and raised a breach of privilege issue against the Prime Minister Rajiv Gandhi and the Defence Minister K.C. Pant. It was obvious that middlemen were involved in the deal and commission was paid. The new evidence revealed that Rajiv Gandhi and K.C. Pant had misled the Parliament and therefore their statements in the House constituted a breach of privilege.

Thereafter, from time to time, I secured a number of documents that provided additional evidence to the Parliament. Ultimately, from various judgements and committee reports it became quite clear that there were middlemen and commissions were paid.

We boycotted the Parliamentary Committee on Bofors because the terms of reference, which we wanted, were not incorporated. I led the move for a boycott. All the four speeches of mine have been included in a small booklet 'Bofors Payoff'.

I think the Prime Minister was misguided, as his initial statement and later turn of events indicate .

I have heard that some of his advisors had warned him not to go to the extent of denying the existence of middlemen and commissions. He preferred bravado to caution.

17

National Front Government

Formation of the National Front government headed by V.P. Singh

V.P. Singh was attracting large audiences throughout the country during the election campaign. We had already formed a National Front. We received a good majority in the election. At that time N.T. Rama Rao from Andhra Pradesh and L.K. Advani had said, "We will support you, provided V.P. is the Prime Minister". Being the leader of the parliamentary party at that time. I presided over the Janata Dal MPs' meeting held in the Central Hall of Parliament, followed by the National Front meeting. Ours was the largest party, so we had to elect our leader and then the Front would elect their leader. I was in the Chair. I said, "I seek proposal for the Leader of the Party in Parliament." V.P. Singh moved the proposal that Devi Lal should become the Leader. Chandra Shekhar supported it. I was stunned; even I was in the dark! So as the presiding authority, I asked, "Any other proposal [I repeated three times] for the post of Leadership of the Janata Dal in Parliament?" Then I said, "I declare that Devi Lal is elected as Leader of the Party in Parliament." Not a single MP in the hall clapped. They were stunned. Everyone was wondering as to what was going on. The whole country had taken for granted that V.P. would be the Prime Minister. But Chandra

Shekhar had said, "No. It seems a group of leaders met to plan the strategy for election for the Janata Dal Parliamentary Party leader."

Who planned the strategy?

I do not know who planned the strategy. They did not take me into confidence. Then Devi Lal got up and spoke. He declared, "You have honoured me by offering the leadership of the Janata Dal in Parliament but it is not my forte. My choice is Raja Sahib." Devi Lal proposed V.P. Singh's name for leadership and it was seconded by Ajit Singh. Then I put it to vote. I said, "There is only one name after Devi Lal's withdrawal. Is there any other name?" There was nobody. Then I said, "Since there is no other name, I declare that V.P. Singh is elected." Chandra Shekhar was very shrewd. He said, "Madhu, you know the technical term." I said, "As I am a Parliamentarian I did not declare 'he is elected unanimously.' If he is elected without any opposition he is elected nem.con (nemine controdicente). That is unopposed." He was satisfied with my explanation, but he was very angry. He felt that some people played foul with him. He never forgot this sudden turn of events.

My experience as a Finance Minister

As you know, the Bofors controversy ushered in the National Front government. In the National Front government led by Shri Vishwanath Pratap Singh, I was appointed the Finance Minister. After V.P. Singh's government fell, I asked him why he chose me as the Finance Minister. He answered, "While I was in the Congress Party and was holding the Finance portfolio, I was very keenly watching your performance in Parliament. On every financial issue you had a specific point of view, a commitment and an outlook and I felt, 'here is a person who has applied his mind to the financial problems and has a financial perspective.' Therefore it is worthwhile on the basis of his performance in the past in the Opposition to see whether he can take this responsibility."

Since I was entrusted with the responsibility of the Finance Ministry, I was aware of the fact that the Budget was to be presented within a limited framework. The Budget should be such that it would steer the economy in the direction, which I have been pleading for all these years while sitting in the Opposition. I thought deeply as to how my Budget could make a deep impact on that section of the society for which we stand. I felt that I should do something, which would catch the imagination of the country. After presenting my first budget the editorials of newspapers from all over the country, from Kashmir to Trivandrum, acknowledged that the budget reflected the personality and the social commitments of Madhu Dandavate.

When I was in the Finance Ministry, I had to make a few changes. For example, I abolished the Gold Control Act. I recognized that excise inspectors would go to small goldsmiths, point out the real or alleged irregularities and extort money from them. Small goldsmiths were very bitter and had requested for an amendment in the Act. The Act was adopted in 1963 due to the Chinese Aggression in 1962, when we wanted more gold. The Act had lost its usefulness in the present context; hence just amending it did not serve any purpose. It had to be abolished. Morarjibhai had introduced this Act when he was the Finance Minister. He wrote to me, "I had introduced this Bill in the past. I recognize that it now has become out of date but nobody had the courage to abolish it. I congratulate you for taking this bold step."

Making the Right to Work a Fundamental Right was another issue I considered in depth. I considered the consequences of making right to work a fundamental right. If it became an obligation on the State, the State would have to give people employment or ensure unemployment compensation. I remembered the comments of former Finance Minister C.D. Deshmukh, who had pointed out that unemployment figures which are revealed by the Employment Exchange do not present the correct picture because it is only the educated in the urban areas who go and register their names. The real count of people who were unemployed, I knew, was much larger than what was documented. The local governments did not have necessary financial resources to provide unemployment compensation. So I suggested that we would ensure the implementation of this law in a phased manner. I proposed that the government would start its implementation from those rural areas, which were drought prone, or flood prone areas. My budget speech led to a big controversy and even those economists who had not read the speech properly, criticised it.

I was very keen on helping the small farmers. The core demand of the farmers has always been to get remunerative prices for their produce. For years, Indian farmers were not getting remunerative prices and all the policy decisions were taken in an ad hoc manner. There were no well-defined norms for protecting the interests of the farmers. I knew that due to lack of consideration for the needs of the small farmers as well as rural artisans and weavers, they had accumulated debt, which they were unable to repay. They were caught in a debt trap and had no guarantee of remunerative prices for their products. As a result these people lived in perennial poverty. In order to relieve our farmers and artisans from the burden of debt, an assurance was given in the National Front's manifesto that we would provide relief to farmers and artisans who had loans up to 10,000 rupees as on 2 October 1989. I was glad to announce in the House that we were ready to implement the debt relief programme to fulfil our promise to the farmers and artisans. I proposed to make the relief available to borrowers who had taken loans up to 10,000 rupees from public sector banks and regional rural banks.

Some of the bankers said that their banks would be destroyed. Some of our cooperative banks have been sinking because these farmers have defaulted on their loans. I pointed out that those objecting to this proposal, fearing that it would result in the collapse of the banks, did not understand that in the Budget, I had made a provision to pay the banks the amounts they were required to waive.

Anyway, I faced a lot of challenges in the Cabinet. I declared that debt receipt above 10,000 rupees will not be waived. Some members of the Cabinet did not feel the limit of 10,000 rupees would go very far because, "Tractor *bhi nahin aata hai* 10,000 *mein.*" (A farmer cannot even buy a tractor for 10,000 rupees), implying that it was impractical to put a limit of 10,000 on the loan waiver amount. They suggested that waiving of 10,000 rupees should be given to even those who have taken 50,000 rupees. My original proposal was that nothing more than 10,000 rupees would be waived. But this would not be applicable to those who had taken 1 lakh or 50,000 rupees. My argument was, "If one had the capacity to take 50,000 rupees' loan he should not be allowed to take advantage of a scheme meant for the poorer farmers who did not have that amount of credit worthiness in the first place." I made my position clear during my budget speech.

During my tenure as Finance Minister and later as the Deputy Chairman of the Planning Commission, I concentrated on the problem of poverty alleviation. The Lakdawala Committee, appointed to study the methodology of poverty estimation, found problems in poverty estimation and reporting methods. There are two methods by which incomes can be estimated, the NSS (National Sample Survey) and the NAS (National Accounts Statistics). Lakdawala pointed out that the two methods produced two different statistical results. The previous government calculated both the figures and publicly announced lower figures in public to create an impression that the poverty was reduced. This method was given a glorious name 'Adjustment Methodology'. I called it Manipulative Methodology. As an alternative, we developed a new method. The poverty line was defined state-wise and for this purpose, for price index in rural areas, the Consumer Price Index (CPI) for agricultural labour was taken as the basis and for urban areas the weighted mean of the CPI for industrial workers and CPI for non-manual sections were used as the basis. This methodology, recommended by Lakdawala, was slightly modified in 1996. The CPI for industrial workers was taken as the appropriate price index for estimating the urban poverty line. This method is now recognized as Modified Lakdawala Methodology for poverty estimation. The poverty ratios computed on the basis of this methodology were nearer to the ground reality compared to those worked out from the earlier methodology.

I must say that today, the problems of small farmers and artisans have worsened in the new culture of globalization, privatization and liberalization. Developed countries export agricultural products, milk products, flowers, and fruits to India. These countries compete with Indian farmers by lowering the price of their products through subsidies provided by their governments. Hence Indian farmers face unfair competition.

It is pertinent to examine the role of the World Bank at this juncture. No Finance Minister shows the Budget to the World Bank before it is presented to the Parliament, because according to the Constitutional provisions, the Budget before being presented to Parliament is a confidential document. However, maintaining some sort of harmonization between the thinking of the World Bank and that of the government is possible and acceptable. Though as a Finance Minister I have attended meetings with the World Bank, the ideas of the World Bank have never guided my policies. Seminars and meetings with the World Bank experts should not dictate our thoughts. However, I do believe that those Finance Ministers whose thinking is similar to that of the World Bank and the IMF do reflect that influence in their Budget recommendations.

Dealing with Finance Institutions

The Deputy Chairman of the Reserve Bank of India had appointed a committee which had come to the conclusion that proforma for the income and expenditure of the bank was outdated and needed revisions. The old proforma allowed people to hide a number of items of expenditure and as a result, the profits shown in the balance sheets did not reflect the accurate picture of profits. The Deputy Chairman of the Reserve Bank of India had already sent a note to all public sector banks and other banks pointing out that the inadequacies in the design of the proforma was leading to inaccurate reporting of profit and loss.

I will give an example of how this weakness in the system played a role in a major scandal in the financial institutions. There was a famous bank scam in which a well-known broker Harshad Mehta was involved and accused. He went to the State Bank of India and it seems that some of the bank officials told him that the proforma was going to be revised which would have some consequences on the level of profit. High profit would become a marginal profit and marginal profit would become a loss. So something drastic needed be done to boost profits. So they told him to have an informal understanding between themselves. They would give him as much advance as he wanted. He could invest the money in public sector institutions like UTI. These persons put deposits into a public sector bank at a time when the rates were rather low and then sold them when the rates went up. As a result they made huge profits. One former UTI Chairman was also involved in this scandal. I had warned him, "The job of a public sector institution like UTI is not to utilize the money for large scale investment in private sector. A public sector financial institution can provide some investment to companies that need capital for stability, but if you invest in a big way in order to make profit, it is not appropriate." However he continued to do so. Financial organizations like State Bank of India and others promised Harshad Mehta that they would give him any amount of advance. If an advance is to be given to an individual beyond a certain limit, approval of a full meeting of the Board of Management is required. This procedure was not followed in the case of Harshad Mehta and it led to setting up of an enquiry. The entire financial system was collapsing.

To prevent such manipulation of the system, I introduced a new provision during the budget session. The new rule stipulated was that if any public sector financial institution wanted to invest money in the shares of a private or a public company and the amount invested in that company was more than 1 per cent of the equity of that company, then within 24 hours, the institution should announce its identity and declare how much investment had been made. This information helps a common man keep track of how public money is being used. When it is reported in the press that a particular company's share value has increased by 30, 35, or 45 per cent, even a man with an elementary knowledge of share dynamics knows that it is not because of policies of that particular company that the share value has gone up, but because somebody has invested a lot of money suddenly. It is important that the common man knows when the share prices rise on accounts of artificial reasons, so that one makes a personal investment choice with caution.

My officers were aware of my values and principles and they knew I would not succumb to any pressure, so they did not let anybody approach me. My focus as a Finance Minister was to help the weaker sections of the society and to encourage these sections through an institutionalized approach. I will give you an example of how I encouraged fishermen to increase their participation in co-operative ventures.

A week prior to the presentation of the Budget, a large delegation of fishermen gave a memorandum requesting me to take back the increase in the excise on diesel. They had mechanised trawlers and needed diesel. The increase in excise on diesel, they pleaded, made their operations unviable. In my budget I provided relief to all those in the coastal areas and the increase in excise duty on diesel was reduced to zero. Again, experts criticised this move.I explained that my Budget proposal had to be read properly. Only those fishermen, who purchased oil for their trawlers or fishing boats through the Fishermen's Cooperative Society, were entitled to this kind of concession. It is important to understand the side effect of this decision. Various fishermen's cooperative organizations acknowledged that this decision encouraged more fishermen to become members of cooperative societies.

The press called this decision a socialist touch to the Budget. Many people told me that this was not a Budget speech prepared by bureaucrats. I expressed my sources of inspiration at the end of my speech. I said, "This is the essence of pragmatism and the quintessence of the unending quest of the socio-economic experimenters like Mahatma Gandhi, JP and Acharya Narendra Deva."

The Congress Party returns to Power

Chandra Shekhar has been a very good friend, but after the collapse of V.P. Singh's government, he left the Janata Party and formed another Party. Rajiv Gandhi assured him his support and the Government was formed under his leadership. Later Rajiv Gandhi withdrew support to the government on trivial grounds, much like his mother did with Charan Singh. It was alleged by the Congress party that a couple of constables from Haryana were spying on Rajiv Gandhi's residence. On this pretext the MPs belonging to the Congress party stayed away from the House when the Motion of Thanks to the President's Address was to be placed before the House and Chandra Shekhar found that his government was in the minority.

Two Motions came up before the House when the switchover from V.P. Singh to Chandra Shekhar took place. The first was a No-Confidence Motion initiated by L.K. Advani against the previous V.P. Singh government. On behalf of the government, V.P. Singh replied to the debate. Advani's resolution was carried. The No-Confidence motion was passed and then the confidence motion for Chandra Shekhar was moved. Since Chandra Shekhar's government was installed by the President's decision he was also to take the Confidence Vote. I was informed by V.P. Singh, "I have piloted the first debate. Now you be our first speaker on Chandra Shekhar's motion of Confidence." I remember, I spoke immediately after Chandra Shekhar moved the Confidence Motion. I said, "I am the saddest man today." Some Congressmen shouted, "Oh, because you have lost power!" I said, "You will not understand the importance of what I am saying. I am sad not because I am no more the Minister. My anguish is that Chandra Shekhar, with whom I shared association in the freedom struggle and in the Socialist movement, is seeking a Vote of Confidence and I have to oppose him! This is my anguish and sorrow." There was silence in the House. I read out various press clippings about what Chandra Shekhar and Rajiv Gandhi had said about each other. Then I said, that I wanted to warn the Prime Minister while opposing the Confidence Vote that he should not forget the way the Janata government was voted out and then the way the Charan Singh government was thrown out. I said "I can assure you Chandra Shekhar, Rajiv Gandhi is sitting here and he will do the same with you, that his mother did with Charan Singh." After three months, when the issue of the constables in Rajiv Gandhi's house led to the fall of the government, I got up and humorously said, "Some governments have fallen on the question of stability, but this government has fallen on the question of constability!" The whole House burst into laughter.

My relations with Chandra Shekhar were very much estranged on this issue. The obvious motivation behind his actions was power.

National Commission for Women

The office of the Prime Minister sent a message to Pramila Dandavate that her campaign had finally succeeded and that the government was ready to institute the National Commission for Women and appoint her as the first chairperson. This message was informally communicated to her at a time when it was clear that V.P. Singh's government had lost the majority in the Lok Sabha and only a formal adoption of the no-confidence motion against the government had to take place in the House. It would have been inappropriate to accept the appointment from a government that had already lost its majority. She requested me to communicate her refusal to accept the appointment to the Prime Minister. In view of her position in the women's movement, she deserved the position but the democratic norms justify her refusal.

18

New Economic Policy under Narasimha Rao

The way Narasimha Rao became the Prime Minister of this country was peculiar. Personally, I had nothing against him but I wonder whether there was any democratic decision of his party, since no Parliamentary Party or Parliamentary Board meeting was held at all. It was just suggested that Narasimha Rao should be made the Prime Minister and he became the Prime Minister. He dragged on for the full term.

Narasimha Rao and Vajpayee were the two persons who proved to be good managers in Parliamentary affairs.

Narasimha Rao's colleagues were not prepared to pull him down. In this case, Congressmen felt that this was the last chance for the Congress party to run the government. The arithmetic of the House was such that no other party could replace the government. By virtue of that reality, they were able to continue in power.

Narasimha Rao turned out to be the greatest spokesman of globalization, liberalization and privatization. I do not think he was able to make any powerful plea in the House in favour of the New Economic Policy (NEP). His tone used to be apologetic. He would say that he considered himself to be a man with scientific perspective. The progress of science and technology was giving a new thrust to the affairs of the world. So how could we lag behind?

Globalization, liberalization and privatization have become the new faith of the world economy and we could not discard it. During his regime, the stock market scams and many other scams surfaced. Even then he survived. Later he was also arrested. But by the strange logic of circumstances, he was let scot-free.

They had appointed Dr Manmohan Singh as the Finance Minister. He had total commitment to the NEP, which in essence meant globalization, liberalization and privatization and overall commitment to the perspective of the WTO. I am not individually challenging his honesty, but the fact is that Manmohan Singh was the Secretary-General of the South Commission established under the chairmanship of Julius K. Nyerere in 1987 and the report of the South Commission under the caption 'Challenge to the South' was submitted in May 1990. When this was pointed out in Parliament, all that Manmohan Singh had to say was that one had the right to change.

One of the reasons why Narasimha Rao did not strike a very strong stand against globalization was because Manmohan Singh dominated the economic policy of the government. At that time Narasimha Rao did not want to clash with Manmohan Singh. So that is how things continued.

We find that Manmohan Singh in a way had become a backbencher, as far as the Rao government was concerned. It must be observed that though he was a vigorous champion of the NEP in the past, with the then prevalent situation of increasing unemployment, ruination of agriculture, closing of industries and growing poverty, he could not have continued the old aggressive thrust to defend the NEP. Having worked with the World Bank and the IMF, his thinking was based on the approach of liberalization, privatization and globalization and he was also in the Planning Commission.

Despite these problems he remained committed to that perspective of the NEP. I want this statement of Narasimha Rao to go on record. I am quoting him:

> *Whatever I might have said earlier, now I feel*
> *that disinvestment of the profit-making public sector*
> *is like selling the bricks of walls of our own house*
> *to pay our grocers' bills.*

Thinking about the present policy of disinvestment in the public sector, it can be said that such disinvestment means partial privatization of the public sector. That means asking the private companies to purchase the shares of the public sector. Private companies will purchase shares of only those public sector organizations which are profit-making public sectors, so that part of the profits can be acquired. What happens with the public sectors that do not make profits? Nobody would try to purchase the shares of those organizations. Thus this process can be described as privatization of profits and nationalization of losses.

The policy of liberalization

I have very strong views on the new economic policy, which really is the policy of globalization, liberalization and privatization. In the 1990s the new orientation of economic perspective was described as economic reform. Later on, it was called the *new economic policy* and its further nomenclature was *structural adjustments in the economy*, but in essence this aspect meant policy of globalization, liberalization and privatization. My views on this subject are not influenced by any dogmatic perspective, but reflect the economic interests of our country and those of the poor developing nations.

In fact, the very concept of developed countries and developing countries flows out of the context of colonialism. The countries from where raw materials and other resources were actually looted remained underdeveloped or developing nations, and the countries to which these resources were transported in course of time became developed countries. Of course, this balance changed slightly at a later stage. Historically, colonialism was behind the division of the world into developing and developed spheres.

We are often told that in an age of science and technology, the spirit of universalism must dominate all our policies and perspectives and that globalization, liberalization and privatization are a part of the new spirit of universalism in this age. For a person like me, who has taught Nuclear Physics for twenty-five years, it is very important to address some of the fallacies in this argument.

I would like to make a distinction between science and technology. Science is undoubtedly universal in character. For instance, the principle of gravitation is applicable in any part of the world, whereas assimilation of modern technology has largely depended on economic and social conditions in different countries. Those who are the beneficiaries of the economic or social order are also greater beneficiaries of the technological advancements.

Mahatma Gandhi's thoughts are relevant in this area. Mahatma Gandhi struck a balance between local and global perspectives. He had once said, "I think universally, but I act locally." I think that is the most important view. Now, I will illustrate the point that technology is not an absolute concept like science and that it must be seen relative to the social and economic conditions. Once, a delegation consisting of some MLAs, MPs and representatives of sugar cooperatives travelled to different parts of the world to study the sugar technology in those countries. They went to Brazil and they asked, "What is your production of sugar in a season?" The answer was, "It is six million tons." Then the next question the delegation asked was, "What is the total labour that is required to produce these six million tons of sugar?" The reply was, "230 employees." Then the person responding to the question clarified, " Actually 230 are not involved in the direct production of sugar, 50 per cent of them are transport and security employees." Only 115 people were required in that unit in Brazil to produce six million tons of sugar in a season. Then the delegation visited cooperative sugar factories in India and compared the impact of technology on production capacity by asking a question, "If 6 million tons or 60 lakh tons of sugar are to be produced per season, what is the strength of the employees that will be required in your factories?" The answer was, "10,000 employees at our level of technology." The next question the MPs asked was, "If you induct the Brazilian technology in which 115 employees produce 6 million tons, what will be net results on your factory?" The immediate response of the Indian sugar factory representatives was, "It is obvious that if the Brazilian technology needs 115 workers to produce 6 million tons and we require 10,000 employees, then when that particular technology is inducted in our country or in this sugar factory, out of 10,000 only 115 employees will be retained and the rest of the workers will be retrenched."

Now that shows how the degree of technology or the level of technology is correlated to the problems of employment, poverty, and production. You cannot think about introducing technology without considering the social factors like poverty, and needs of employment.

Science is universal in concept, but technology must be viewed within the framework of time and space. Having stated this, now let us go to the WTO. The Marakesh (in Morocco) Agreement of the GATT (General Agreement on Tariff and Trade) came into effect on 1 January 1995. Subsequent events represent how globalization, liberalization and privatization have had a disastrous impact on the economies of the poorer countries. I believe that the impact will be more pronounced in the future.

To substantiate my point let me give you the example of India. The developed countries give large-scale internal financial assistance to the producers of agriculture products. In addition, they are given export subsidies for exporting their products to poor and developing countries such as India. For example, in the United States of America, the internal financial assistance given to the agricultural products is of the order of 47 billion dollars. In addition to that, the government offers enormous export subsidies, to make American agricultural produce competitive in the world market. When these products land in the markets of poor countries like India or any other countries of Asia, Africa or Latin America, they enjoy unfair advantage over the local farmers.

I fear the worst from the effects of WTO on the poor countries such as India. We cannot forget that the Indian economy is based on agriculture. I want to first address the impact of WTO policies on the agriculture sector in India because the acid test of any economic policy in India lies in its impact on the agriculture sector. The agriculturists in this country constitute about 65-70 per cent of the population. In India 30 to 35 percent of the Gross Domestic Product (GDP) is contributed by agriculture and the related services, and 60 to 65 per cent of employment in the country is also generated in the agriculture sector. You cannot ignore the contribution of the agriculture sector to the Indian economy. It is important to keep in mind the basic minimum need of the agriculturists in our country. The peasant demands remunerative prices for agricultural produce. The inputs such as fertilizers, equipment and other resources required for production and transportation are increasingly becoming expensive. With increase in the cost of electricity, those who utilize electric pumps find that the cost of irrigation has gone up as well. While the cost of agricultural production has become more and more expensive, the price offered to the agriculturists for their produce is not remunerative. Many variables have to be considered in ensuring remunerative prices for the agriculturists. Even a slight variation in the cost of inputs such as manure, fertilizers, electricity, and seeds can have an impact on how remunerative the agricultural product is. The Indian farmers are constantly struggling to earn their living in an ever escalating cost structure.

In this scenario, the entry of subsidized produce from developed countries is only adding to the hardships of Indian agriculturists. As a consequence of WTO regulations there is an inflow of cheap agricultural products such as flowers, fruits, etc. into the Indian market. These products destroy the markets of the agriculturists in India leading to deprivation of opportunities for livelihood. I want to repeat that a larger employment is provided by agriculture and related services in India. If this sector is destroyed, it will destroy the economy of the country, leading to spread of poverty. In a developing country like India, eradication of poverty has to be one of the key priorities. In the Ninth Plan, which we formulated, I emphasized that the first Plan priority has to be agriculture and related services. I want to warn that inflow of cheap agricultural products from developed countries will destroy the domestic market for Indian agriculturists. When the agriculturist does not get remunerative prices, the agricultural labour does not get adequate wages, not even minimum wages. This is a very important aspect that has to be taken note of while thinking about globalization.

Earlier, imports into India were restricted by quantitative restrictions. Since April 1,2001, these restrictions have disappeared. During the debate over quantitative restrictions government said that originally quantitative restrictions were introduced because it affected our foreign exchange reserves. They are now justifying removal of the restrictions in the light of improvement in the foreign exchange reserves. The ground reality is by removing the quantitative restrictions on exports from developed countries to poorer countries like India, it has become easier for developed countries to use their internal assistance such as high export subsidies to increase flow of agricultural produce into our country. This is my big concern.

Despite a concerted campaign by the critics of WTO policies, a lot of manipulations are going on. As per the conditions of the WTO, for developed and developing countries, there is a percentage limit for subsidies. Now, to escape that clause some of the developed countries show a part of the subsidy as the research and consulting expenditure incurred by the government (as opposed to declaring it as a subsidy). The trade ministers of 146 member-countries of the WTO met in Cancun from 10th to 14th September, 2003, where the main issue before the delegation was to review the agreement on agriculture (AoA), first arrived at the Uruguay Round of the erstwhile GATT. The commitment to reduce subsidies under the AoA was restricted to the amber box subsidies only. However I already see serious breach of these rules as developed nations start circumventing the rules by redesigning an amber box subsidy into a blue or green box.

(The term 'Amber box' 'Blue box' and the 'Green box' are WTO jargon. Amber box indicates trade distorting domestic support, primarily by encouraging excess production. The blue box subsidies are somewhat less trade distorting, because while they directly link production to subsidies, they also set limits on production e.g. quotas. The green box is considered minimally trade distorting. A good example of green box subsidies would be direct income support schemes unlinked to production.)

There is also a move amongst the developed countries to reduce the land under cultivation in developing countries. To achieve this goal developed countries are even willing to offer peasants assistance as an incentive for cultivating less land.

There is another aspect to be considered. If you look at the figures presented in the Parliament, in this new climate of globalization and liberalization, it is the small-scale industry that has suffered the most. Again from the perspective of generating employment, I am a strong supporter of small-scale industries. Even the Finance Minister, who was a supporter of globalization, had said in one of his budget speeches, "40 per cent of the total manufacturing capacity in this country comes from the small scale-sector. Then 40 per cent of the exports also come from the small-scale industry. Substantial foreign exchange is also gained by the small-scale sector and this sector at one time provided employment to about a crore of people."

I would like to quote an answer, which was given in Rajya Sabha. According to information supplied by the Minister in reply to an Unstarred Question in Rajya Sabha on 13 March, 2000, "In 1997, 1998, and in 1999, totally 7,62,789 small scale sector units were rendered sick." The corresponding number of non small-scale sector units, which were sick in a year before the process of liberalization took root, was 7,636. If you compare approximately 7,000 large sector units that were closed down with more than 7 lakh small scale units that have come down during the liberalization period, you can get a sense of the impact of liberalization in terms of unemployment.

I want to represent my views on problem of liberalization and globalization in terms of the human sufferings and human misery. I am quoting the figures that were given on the floor of Parliament. Therefore one important effect is large-scale unemployment and poverty.

I would also like to discuss privatization. In the entire framework of the new economic policy, privatization has become the key word. I want to point out another interesting fact. The World Bank, which is supposed to help development through credit, has a separate department called the Department for the Promotion of Privatization. I do not think it is the business of the World Bank to prescribe what should be the model of the policy of development. Development policy has to be framed according to indigenous factors. By setting up an official Department for the Promotion of Privatization it has made its bias known. The global institutions of

World Bank and the IMF are being used to enforce the ideas of privatization, liberalization and globalization, which as I explained earlier, work against the national priorities of generating employment and eliminating poverty. As a result these financial institutions are not serving their mandate for promoting development.

Before the disinvestment process was begun, there was a Disinvestment Commission that was set up. Even that Commission, which was committed to the process of disinvestment, warned that if at all disinvestment in the public sector takes place, precaution should be taken to see that the accruals from the disinvestment are used to strengthen social sectors, and not for reducing fiscal deficit. The remaining available resources should be used to strengthen the weaker public sectors. These norms recommended by the Disinvestment Commission have been totally ignored once the disinvestment process has began.

Often a question is posed to the opponents of the liberalization process: "If all this process of globalization, liberalization and privatization on which the WTO is actually based is against the interest of developing countries, then why did so many other developing countries accept them?" I can give an answer to this question. Most of the developing countries expected that a strong country like India, which is also a developing country, would play the role of the watchdog against the impact of globalization, liberalization and privatization. But when India agreed to sign it, then willy-nilly others followed suit. I am sorry that rather than fighting the WTO's wrong policies and avoiding the damage that is being done, India decided to join the agreement.

There is another aspect that I want to cover in my argument. Some people, especially those who benefit from the rising tide of opposition to globalization, liberalization and privatization, argue that the meeting of the Commerce Ministers in Doha has contributed a lot in easing the tension between the developed and developing countries. It is true that at the Doha Conference of the Commerce Ministers, late Murasoli Maran, who represented India, pointed out, "While reframing the policy in the next round, you should see to it that sovereign rights of the countries to frame their own policies in certain sectors is not at all jeopardized. There are certain sectors, which you should not take up." But this point was not recorded as a dissent in the minutes. When the leaders of the WTO found that there were a lot of controversies around this issue, they found a way out. They decided not to have the formal next Round. It was argued that three fields, investment, procurement by the government and competitive policy, would not be taken up for discussion for two years. In the meanwhile it was decided to create a 'Work Programme', not the final policy document, and that after two years the regular round of negotiations would start. It is important that the developing countries are not complacent about the Work Programme. WTO has also set up a Trade Negotiations Committee. This is an organizational instrument, which is usually required for carrying on the formal negotiations. There is no guarantee that investment, competitive policy and procurement will be completely kept out of the work programme. I am sure that these issues will be considered in the Work Programme. My hunch is that there are issues on which there is great resentment, particularly in the developing countries, and for two years the discussions and controversies will be avoided and the Work Programme machinery will work. The very items, which are objected to, will be also discussed informally and after two years, they will plead that informally these have already been discussed and so all parties should agree to put a stamp of approval at the formal Round. So the Work Programme will be converted into the programmes of the next round of negotiations. That is likely to happen. Developing countries need to watch.

The new economic policy will not only mean liberalization of imports, but also inviting multi-nationals to take over our industries. The government is even inviting foreign companies into the Insurance sector. The multinational companies do not have a commitment to generating employment in the country. Wherever multi-nationals have been formed, they first take a review of how many workers in a particular unit are nearing retirement. Those that have about 5-7 years left before their retirement are told that they would be given a cheque equalling their monthly salary on the first day of every month for all the years remaining before their retirement. A lot of workers find the opportunity of earning a salary without working very attractive. They do not realize that the real motivation behind this offer is to permanently reduce the number of people employed in the unit. It has been a tradition in India that nearer to the point of retirement every employee looks forward to passing on his job to his son or a close relative. However, under the new economic circumstances, those seeking early retirement lose this opportunity to create employment for his or her son. Multinationals want to rationalize production and achieve efficiencies and profitability by replacing labour with technology. That is how unemployment will grow and along with that the problem of poverty will also grow.

If you look at the rural and semi-urban areas there are very few heavy industries. These areas only have cottage and small-scale industries. As mentioned earlier, as a result of liberalization, many of the small scale and cottage industries have closed down leading to increase in poverty. In such a situation people like us, who have always fought for protecting the rights of the poor, will need to organize a constructive struggle against unemployment, rising poverty and the new economic policies.

Against this background I want to share a big concern I have about the apathy of the middle class towards the suffering of the poor. I want to compare the psychological atmosphere in the country during the pre-Independence days with the mindset of the middle class in a liberalized economy. In the past whenever various struggles were undertaken under the leadership of Mahatma Gandhi or of Kisan Sabhas or Kisan Panchayats, there was an atmosphere of support from the middle class. Even the upper classes had sympathy for people's struggles.

The Dandi March for salt or the peasants' agitation in Kheda organized by Mahatma Gandhi, the No-Tax Campaign under the leadership of Vallabhbhai in Bardoli and the Champaran Satyagraha attracted large-scale support and participation of the middle classes.

I will narrate an interesting episode. In the pre-Independence era, there was a milk product company called Polson. Polson was purchasing milk from villagers at throwaway prices and making huge profits. Tragically enough, they were given a special license by the then Bombay Government for its milk distribution scheme. Then during the War, the Polson Company was given the sole monopoly of supplying cream and butter to the British army. The peasants from Kheda district demanded that Polson must purchase their milk at more remunerative prices, when they were earning huge profits. But they could not get their demands met. So the villagers started pouring their milk down the streets. At that time, Vallabhbhai Patel sent Morarjibhai Desai to Kheda district. He collected all the small milk producers and advised them that "throwing away the milk would not help achieve their demands. They must force the Polson Company and other purchasers to give you a remunerative price for their milk and must organize a cooperative milk diary so that at good prices they can directly supply milk products to the consumers".

The villagers approached the Bombay State government. The Deputy Milk Commissioner doubted if rustic villagers who had no understanding or knowledge of Technology could ever run milk cooperatives. In response the villagers started pouring milk on the streets for a number of days. Then the Deputy Milk Commissioner met the strikers and gave them the permission to form a cooperative. That is how the milk producers' cooperatives grew. During this agitation, the villagers had the sympathy of different sections of the society. The ordinary people recognized that by supporting the demands of the milk producers, they would get milk products at a good price and were assured of better quality.

Now, there is a psychological change in the new atmosphere of globalization, privatization and liberalization, even among the middle classes. There is hardly any recognition of and participation in the fight on issues such as land reforms, employment and poverty. The middle class has surrendered its responsibility to lead the fight against poverty and inequality in our society. They feel they have nothing to gain or lose by supporting such struggles. It is none of their concern. This is the prevailing attitude.

So the new middle class, who believes in consumerism, is just not worried about what happens to the poor, peasants, and the unemployed.

The emergence of this new class is quite visible all over India. This is a new culture that has developed. I am talking not in terms of city dwellers; I am talking about the upper middle and higher classes. Their psychology is, "I will serve the new businesses owned by the multi-nationals. You may fight your battle; I want to make sure that I make a lot of money." This is the new mindset.

In the midst of this consumerist culture, the toiling, suffering masses, the poor, the unemployed, will now have to carry the burden of fighting for their just rights on their own shoulders, because the middle class has given up its historic responsibility of being the voice of the deprived sections. Even on economic issues, the middle and poor classes were united during the pre-independence era. That unity has now been disrupted and the poor are forced to fight on their own. The heritage of the freedom struggle has been squandered away.

In fact, I never used labels like a 'Nehruvian pattern' of economy. I believe in a pattern of economy in which economic and political models will subserve the interest of the process of devolution of power and de-centralization of economy which in turn will subserve the aims of economic equality and social justice. I would like to recall my observations on the day of the release of the biography of the famous economist P.C. Mahalanobis, who founded the Indian Statistical Institute. Mahalanobis is known as a strong proponent of centralized planning. While outlining the importance of decentralized planning process I said, "Mahalanobis had a scientific mind and deep understanding of the needs of development. Keeping in view the present circumstances, even if he were to be alive today he would have probably supported my advocacy of decentralized planning."

We must understand that when India attained independence our immediate need was to build infrastructure that would support development. At that time, the focus was on establishing heavy industries, and strong infrastructure. The process of decentralization was not adequately supported. In fact, when the final draft of the Constitution was prepared, some Gandhians went to President Rajendra Prasad and said, "Throughout the text of the Constitution, the words 'Panchayati Raj Institution' are not used. Does that mean that we are ending the process of decentralization?" The concept of Panchayati Raj may not have been incorporated originally into the Constitution in the form in which Gandhi pleaded, but then it has to be evolved. Process of devolution of power in the decentralized economy is a necessity. There must be more economic and political powers at the grass-roots level, so that the gains of development are not monopolized by the creamy layers to their neglect.

On their intervention, for the first time in the Directive Principles of State Policies, the Article 40 regarding the Panchayati Raj Institutions was incorporated. Then, as the thinking on this topic evolved, the 73rd and 74th Amendment Bills provided further clarity on this aspect. With these amendments the concept of de-centralization gained constitutional endorsement, though it did not receive adequate thrust in the planning process. Jawaharlal Nehru held the reigns of power immediately after the British rule. It was a period when there was terrible destruction everywhere in the country; the economy was in shambles and political life had to be stabilized. At that time Nehru faced the compulsions of investing in heavy industries. These were compulsions of the time. That does not mean that the pattern called the Nehruvian pattern must continue in the same form ignoring the needs of the grass roots. Every pattern has to evolve in keeping with the needs of the time and therefore to my mind, this debate, whether the Nehruvian pattern is relevant or not, is outdated.

In fact, I want to go on record to say [I said it in Parliament, when I was a Finance Minister and also the Deputy Chairman of the Planning Commission]: "The model of development in this country and the economic policies of the country will have to be viewed in the context of the constraints in our economy such as inadequacy of capital, large unemployment and poverty, rural backwardness and lack of appropriate technology."

When we take these constraints into account, we realize that our model cannot be a uni-dimensional model of development. Therefore to overcome all these constraints in our economy, our model will have to combine the efforts of the institutions from the public, private and cooperative sectors. What name one would give to that model is of little relevance. What is significant is that the content and utilization of this model must help remove imbalance and inequalities in the Indian society. We have to ensure that we do not depend on a trickle-down model of development, which will result in concentration of resources at the top, with those at the lower rung waiting endlessly with begging bowls to collect the trickle-down gains of development.

I would say that stress on decentralization in political and economic spheres is necessary and therefore a new pattern with emphasis on decentralization has to evolve. It does not matter which party rules the country. If the problems and the constraints to which I have made a reference are to be addressed, then a new model that combines various sectors of economy is needed.

19

Rise of Communalism

The Babri Masjid and after

Prior to the demolition of the Babri Masjid the Chief Minister of Uttar Pradesh had assured to the Supreme Court, Parliament and National Integration Council that the structure of the Babri Masjid at Ayodhya would be fully protected.

However in the presence of the prominent leaders of the BJP, some members of the congregation of sadhus and their supporters assembled at Ayodhya, mounted the Babri Masjid and demolished its structure. This happened in the presence of the State Police, who were ordered to withdraw from the scene. The police and the state administration of U.P. had abdicated their responsibility. They remained silent spectators of the demolition of the Mosque. This constituted a serious breach of the assurance given to the Supreme Court, Parliament and National Integration Council by the then Chief Minister of U.P.

Demolition of the Babri Masjid became a watershed in Indian politics. It exposed the most aggressive communal forces at the forefront. The communal forces took maximum political advantage from the emerging situation. Those who had remained marginalized for years in the nation's politics made a great leap forward. These forces sought to replace the spirit of tolerance, which was the essence of India's composite culture, by fanaticism and communal hatred. The demolition of the Babri Masjid brought about the alienation of Muslims and other minorities from the mainstream of the nation's political and social life. This was a severe blow to secularism, which was assiduously nurtured during India's freedom struggle and various social and cultural movements.

For a secularist like me this was the greatest damage done to India's image as a secular state. However I would not lose hope. In the evolution of the world there have been varying periods of time like the stone age, medieval age, dark ages, renaissance and a golden age. Why should we be unnerved by the present phase of rising communalism? People have to be mobilized against communalism as well as against economic and social injustice. People must be made to realize that the communalists, through diversionary tactics, will only weaken the social and economic struggles of the deprived sections of the society. Restoring the secular spirit is an uphill task, but there is no alternative except to fight back the monster of communalism and preserve the secular foundations of our Constitution.

20

United Front Government

I became the Deputy Chairman of the Planning Commission when Deve Gowda became the Prime Minister in 1996. I want to emphasize that during various phases in my political life, the freedom struggle, Goa liberation struggle, during anti-Emergency movement and other struggles, and as a Minister, my approach, philosophy and perspective remained the same and that was to voice the problems of peasants, working class, and the youth. When I took over as the Deputy Chairman of the Planning Commission, many people commented to me that the role of the Planning Commission had been undermined for many years. My efforts were to re-vitalize the Planning Commission. When the Chief Ministers of various States came to see me, we had a full-fledged meeting with them, with all our experts and all members of the Planning Commission. Once a CPI (M) leader told me, "No matter what the ideological orientation of the Chief Minister is, everyone is happy after meeting you, since you are sensitive to the situation of the States and provide maximum possible benefit you can."

During my tenure, the Ninth Five-Year Plan was formulated. It was a matter of pride that my colleagues and I tried to give a new thrust to the Ninth Plan, which was consistent with the philosophy and the ideals we cherished for a long time.

During my Deputy Chairmanship of the Planning Commission the most important change we brought about was in the methodology adopted to measure poverty. We also involved groups of NGOs, trade unions, peasant organizations and voluntary organizations in the planning process. As a part of the decentralization process, we often reached out to the States to discuss their problems and ideas. We assigned specific responsibilities for incorporating the ideas from these interactions in the plan document to various individuals within the Commission. I opted to draft the first chapter 'Perspective, Objectives and Strategy of Development' and the 'Procedure for the Finalisation of the Plan.'

The first step was consultations within the National Development Council, which is headed by the Chairperson of the Planning Commission. The National Development Council includes all the Chief Ministers and Finance Ministers of the Union Government.

National Development Council helped prepare the Approach Document to the Ninth Five-Year Plan mentioning the priorities. The National Development Council adopted the Approach Paper to the Ninth Five-Year Plan on 16 January 1997. It provided a broad framework to the plan. Specifically it outlined overall objectives and emerging issues, macro level vision of the plan, development strategy, policy priorities, sectoral strategies, perspective of cooperative federalism, the nature of implementation and delivery system. Another important aspect of the Approach Document was that it clearly defined the priorities of the Plan as:

> *Priority to agriculture and rural development*
> *with a view to generating adequate productive*
> *employment and eradication of poverty;*

> *Accelerating the growth rate of the economy*
> *with stable prices;*

> *Ensuring food and nutritional security for all,*
> *particularly, the vulnerable sections of society;*

> *Providing the basic minimum services of safe*
> *drinking water, primary health care facilities, universal*

*primary education, shelter and conductivity to all in a
time-bound manner;*
  *Containing the growth rate of population;
ensuring environmental sustainability of the
development process through social mobilization and
 participation of people at all levels;*

  *Empowerment of women and socially
disadvantaged groups, such as, Scheduled Castes,
Scheduled Tribes and other Backward Classes,
Minorities as agents of economic change and
development;*

  *Promoting and developing people's
participatory institutions like Panchayati Raj
institutions, Cooperatives and Self-Help groups; and
 strengthening efforts to build Self-Reliance.*

In the second step, the Planning Commission broadened its consultations and approached various institutions (outside of the National Development Council and the state governments) and prepared a Draft Plan based on the input received from the new round of consultations.

The final step was to share the Draft Plan with the cabinet and secure its approval, after which it would become the official Five-Year Plan Document.

We completed all this work, but I was very unhappy that after burning the midnight oil, the government lost its majority. During this period even the National Development Council became ineffective due to instability in many of the State governments. Additionally due to the political instability at the centre, even the cabinet could not approve it. The framework of the Approach Paper provided the objectives, emerging issues, macro dimensions of the Plan, development strategy and policy priorities, sectoral strategies, perspective of cooperative federalism and the nature of implementation and delivery system. The Approach Paper projected a 7 per cent annual G.D.P. growth scenario with necessary targets of domestic saving rate, current account deficit, incremental capital output ratio, investment rate and total plan size of 8,75,000 crore rupees. The Internal Planning Commission, not the full Planning Commission, undertook the exercise of working out the details of the Ninth Plan within the framework of the Approach Paper adopted by the National Development Council consistent with the spirit of cooperative federalism. The views of the State governments and the Panchayati Raj institutions were sought through consultations and serious consideration was given to them during the formulation of the Draft Ninth Five-Year Plan. As the work of preparing the Draft Ninth Plan was at the concluding stage, the political events certainly overtook the planning process when the Lok Sabha was dissolved and the General Elections were announced. In this new situation due to inadequacy of time available, it became difficult to get the Ninth Plan approved by the full Planning Commission, the Union Cabinet and the National Development Council. Therefore, in consultation with the Chairman of the Planning Commission, that is Prime Minister, it was thought advisable that consistent with our commitment to transparency and accountability to the people, the Draft Plan prepared by the Internal Planning Commission should be published. It could be utilized as input for the Ninth Five-Year Plan to be finalized by the new government installed after the Lok Sabha elections and placed before the National Development Council for adoption. It was hoped that the publication of this Draft Ninth Plan would help in sustaining continuity of the planning process.

One of the bureaucrats who were associated with our Cabinet, issued a public statement criticising my decision to go public with the document, He said, "The next Government will view this decision as a hostile act and it would be difficult to get it passed smoothly."

I was very careful. I had consulted the Prime Minister, taken his written sanction and then made it public.

Fortunately, for me and unfortunately for that bureaucrat who publicly criticized me, I was proved right and he was proved wrong. The new government, adopted the entire Plan document as it was; only in respect of the plan outlay of 8,50,000 crore rupees, they made a slight change. I recall telling one of the Ministers in the next government, " Well, I am thankful to you that you adopted our Plan as it is. In fact, you have not even corrected the spelling mistakes from our draft." I did not want our Planning Commission only to wag the tail, but I wanted to push some of the bold initiatives we had conceptualized in our Plan by inviting a public debate. This was the main reason for which I disregarded the opinion of some officials inside the Planning Commission who were wavering. I put my foot down and said, "I am strongly of the opinion that we should release it. We have worked so hard for about one and a half years. Let it go before the people and the new government. If they reject it, let them. The new government accepted our plan.

I would like to narrate another interesting event that occurred during my tenure at the Planning Commission. It was the year of Subhas Chandra Bose's birth centenary. On the first day, after taking over as the Deputy Chairman, I narrated to my colleagues how Subhas Babu had played a great role in the planning process. Netaji Subhas Chandra Bose in his Presidential Address had first outlined the need for planning as a corner stone of economic reconstruction of free India at the Haripura Session of the Indian National Congress held in February 1938. In his address Netaji envisaged that the first task of the Government of Free India would be to set up a National Planning Committee. Having talked about the importance of National Planning at Haripura in February 1938, Netaji inaugurated a National Planning Committee on 17 December 1938. He appointed Pandit Jawaharlal Nehru as the first Chairman of this Committee. This National Planning Committee later was succeeded by the Advisory Planning Board set up by the Interim Government in 1946. Subsequently, in free India, the Planning Commission, as it is known today, was constituted in 1950. Subhas Chandra Bose was the pioneer of Indian Planning. He even declined to be the Chairman of the Committee by saying, "I am the President of the Congress and the party President should not become the Chairman of that Committee."

21

Estimation of Poverty

I used to focus on the problems of poverty and methodology for estimation of poverty even before I took over as Deputy Chairman of the Planning Commission. I found ample opportunity during my tenure as Deputy Chairman of the Planning Commission to study and discuss this problem in depth. I also tried to find out what the earlier methods regarding estimation of poverty were and what the lacunae were and how they needed to be corrected so that we could have a method of estimation of poverty, which provided a real picture.

The year 2001 was the Centenary Year of Professor D.R. Gadgil, who was, earlier, the Deputy Chairman of the Planning Commission. I wrote an article titled 'Fifty Years of Planning in India.' One of the important aspects of the planning process in India has been to evolve a methodology for poverty estimates and to ascertain, correspondingly, the extent of the population living below the poverty line. In this context, defining the poverty line was a basic task.

In 1962 a working group of economists suggested that on the basis of minimum diet prescribed by the Indian Council of Medical Research (ICMR) in 1958, as per capita monthly expenditure at 1960-61 prices, this could be worked out as 20 rupees per month for rural and 25 rupees per month for urban areas. Those with income less than this were considered to be living below the poverty line.

In 1971, economists V.M. Dandekar and Nilakantha Rath proposed a food basket providing 2,250 calories per capita per day as the basis for estimating the poverty line. Using data from the 1960-61 consumer expenditure survey by the National Sample Survey (NSS) and taking into account a minimum non-food expenditure, Dandekar and Rath recommended 15 rupees per capita per month (for rural) and 22.5 rupees per capita per month (for urban) as the poverty line at 1960-61 prices. The contribution made by Dandekar and Rath earlier was the consideration of the food basket only but presently some other minimum non-food expenditure like education, etc., was also considered. This meant that those who were able to get this particular amount were just on the borderline and those who were below this line were poor.

The next important shift took place in 1979. The Task Force of the Planning Commission used data from the 28th Round of the National Sample Survey (NSS) 1973-74 and on the basis of minimum calories of 2,400 per capita per day for rural areas and 2,100 calories for urban areas, suggested that expenditure of 49.1 rupees per capita per month (for rural) and 56.6 rupees per capita per month (for urban) as the cut-off lines for poverty estimation and called this the Traditional Methodology.

The Planning Commission's Expert Group in 1989 headed by Professor Lakdawala corrected the inaccuracies in the Traditional Methodology of the Task Force and suggested a Modified Methodology for poverty estimation. I have already referred to the Traditional Methodology, and that is that both the NSS method and the NAS (National Account Statistics) methods were used and in whichever the poverty shown was less, it was accepted. As a result accurate poverty estimation was not done. Professor Lakdawala objected. He called it wrong and unethical. He suggested, "Unadjusted Methodology should be used when there is no manipulation; poverty line cannot be unique for the whole country as there is a poverty variation from State to State. Therefore, one must work out the poverty line for each State by the common methodology." For urban areas the weighted mean of the Consumer

Price Index (CPI) for industrial workers and CPI for non-manual sections was used as the basis. For this purpose, for price index in rural areas, the Consumer Price Index for agriculture labour was taken as the basis. Later on the Lakdawala methodology was slightly modified in 1996. The CPI for industrial workers was taken as the appropriate price index for estimating the urban poverty line. This is generally described as 'Modified Lakdawala Methodology for poverty estimation.' The poverty ratios computed on the basis of this methodology were nearer to accuracy.

For the year 1993-94, on the basis of the earlier 'Adjusted' method the population below the poverty line was 18 per cent whereas according to the Modified Lakdawala Methodology, it was 36 per cent, almost twice, quite close to the ground reality.

During my deputy chairmanship, the Planning Commission had set up a Committee to enquire into the position of the centrally-sponsored schemes. The Committee was asked to find out how many schemes were there, how much funds they had and how many of them could be transferred to the States so that in the process of poverty alleviation, additional opportunities would be made available. The Planning Commission suggested that out of 181 centrally-sponsored schemes with an outlay of Rs.16,000 crore, only those schemes which were of an inter-State nature should be retained as centrally-sponsored schemes. The choice of schemes was left to the States.

In many cases, States and Centre were ruled by different political parties and the States resented the fact that they had to do the resource mobilization at the State level under the terms set by the Centre. It was a psychological barrier.

Often I found bureaucrats cautioning the Chief Ministers by saying, "We would get Rs. 16,000 but we would remain dependent on the Centre." The North-Eastern states had a different approach. They acknowledged the helpful attitude existent during our tenure in the Planning Commission.

During my tenure in the Planning Commission, the government brought focus on the needs of north-east region.

22

Transforming the North-East

We recognized that this resource-rich, northeast region is truly a national asset. The development of its resources such as hydroelectric, oil and gas, coal, bio-diversity and agro-silvicultural potential, hold a promise of a national solution through regional development. We also believed that focus on the development of this region would add to national security in every respect.

To ensure that the north-east region is brought into the national stream, we appointed a commission under the leadership of Mr. S.P. Shukla. The commission was given complete freedom to conduct their investigation. We promised them that if they required more funds to complete their study, then the funds would be made available. S.P. Shukla did an excellent job. He travelled from village to village and talked to people, financial institutions and experts and then prepared a report titled 'Transforming the North-east'. His contribution was highly appreciated by the north-east States.

The report emphasized that the north-east region could not be developed just incrementally but through a quantum leap in resource mobilization. Such an effort needed to be assigned a national priority. The Commission felt that there was a need to end the north-east region's perceived sense of isolation and neglect and to take concrete steps to break the vicious circle of economic stagnation and unemployment. This sense of neglect is the root cause of militancy, which in turn hampers investment. This is why we have not been able to harness the abundant natural resources of this region to their full potential.

The report reminded us that effecting a quantum jump in developmental efforts would require considerable increase in the plan outlay to this region. It proposed building enhanced capacity to develop and implement programmes and projects and setting up of appropriate monitoring mechanisms to preclude leakages as well as time and cost overruns.

Let me state why it is important to monitor time and cost overruns. Suppose the gestation period of a project is five years, but because of lack of timely availability of finances or proper monitoring it extends to nine or ten years, then the delay results in significant increase in the cost of implementation. We need to use limited resources available for development more efficiently by building checks and balances in use of the funds.

The S.P. Shukla Committee recommended that the local, state and central authorities would need to gear themselves to the task and devise more effective norms and systems to ensure results. The North-Eastern Council (NEC) would need radical reorganization, if it were to be a meaningful nodal agency in the new context.

The financial resources needed could not be raised by conventional methods. It was therefore significant that during the Ninth Plan the Prime Minister promised additional funds to the north-east states.

It is important that the rest of the country should better appreciate the unique needs of the north-east region. There is a need for a preferential treatment to the north-east region.

The proposed preferential treatment suggested in the S.P. Shukla Commission's report is justified on the basis of the reality that the region was uniquely disadvantaged by the Partition of India and Pakistan. The Partition left this region's external perimeter with no more than 2 per cent contiguity with the rest of India. The remaining 98 per cent of the land has always faced inhospitable international boundaries. Hardly any other State faces such a situation. Secondly, no part of the country except Jammu and

Kashmir has been driven by prolonged and multiple insurgencies that have held development in this region to ransom. It means that certain percentage of annual allocations made to every State on the basis of set norms by the Planning Commission, should be given to the north-east region.

It is in this context that the Commission headed by S.P. Shukla justifiably appealed to all States in the country to adopt a sympathetic and preferential attitude to the region. Our thrust was to ensure the interests and aspirations of the north-east region in harmony with the nation's overall aspiration for development. Marginalized regions have the potential to play a bigger role in the development of our country.

23

Power Shifts

I will give a general overview of what has happened over the years. If you look at the history of change in governments at the Centre and at the States, you will find that the normal political structure and pattern does not change very much. Generally the political scenario comprises three types of political groupings, the most powerful parties, the middle groups, and marginal groups. Major contribution to the freedom struggle was made by all (including communists) under the banner of Congress in the post-Independence period. Everybody who participated in India's freedom struggle, including Netaji Subhas Chandra Bose, Mahatma Gandhi, Jawaharlal Nehru and others accepted the Indian National Congress as the broadest national front. Mahatma Gandhi repeatedly said that the Congress was not a traditional party. It was a broad national front, an instrument for struggle and a means to secure freedom. He even suggested that once India attained freedom, we should dissolve the Congress and convert it into Lok Sewa Sangh. He believed that after attaining freedom Congress's role would be over. Gandhi indicated that such an ideologically heterogeneous combination could not conduct the administration of a country. The Interim Government was formed in 1946 and the new government took over on 15 August 1947. Later, in 1952, the first general elections were conducted and the first elected government took over. People, who were not originally a part of the Congress but had a great vision, were invited by Jawaharlal Nehru to improve the quality of his administration, for example Dr B.R. Ambedkar. In fact, Gandhiji made it clear that if Dr Ambedkar were not included in the Cabinet, he would not give his support. So, Dr. Ambedkar was brought into the Cabinet. The Cabinet was almost a monolithic structure. The government and the party in power were the same because the new government was a result of the legacy of the freedom struggle. In the post independence era, the Congress party was able to draw upon the goodwill of the prolonged freedom struggle and establish itself as the main party. Many other political groups that have lead freedom struggles around the world enjoy such an advantage. For instance, the famous leader Nelson Mandela led the South African struggle and his party became the major party to lead the new democratic structure in South Africa; Mujibur Rahman emerged as the spokesman of Bangladesh and helped establish the Awami League as its first ruling party.

Gandhi's advice

Mahatma Gandhi once told the Socialist leaders, "You are a strong group within the Congress party. You are a part and parcel of the Congress; you are not an independent party. Be satisfied even with the limited strength you have been able to acquire. Do not imagine that in competition with the Congress, you will get votes and seats though you have substantial voter support." The fortunes of political parties are linked to the pace of political events and popular sentiment of the time. Sudden and unusual events bring about drastic changes. As I mentioned earlier, the Congress during those days was different – the legacy and heritage of freedom struggle, sacrifices, bravery, all had a cumulative effect on the minds of the Indian electorate and the Congress party was the primary beneficiary of that effect.

We left the Congress in 1948, though right from 1930 onwards, we all were there as a part of the Congress in the freedom struggle. People still recognized us as the freedom fighters that carried the Congress flag, the flag of the freedom movement. That image lingered in public psyche. Independent identity of the Socialists could not be built all of a sudden. Within four years of leaving the Congress party in 1948 at the Nasik conference we were faced with elections. We fought the very first election separate from the Congress. We could not match the heritage and tradition of a party that was formed in 1885. The Congress party benefited from this heritage for many years. Honestly, we should not have expected spectacular results in the first elections. However we emerged as the second largest party in terms of votes secured in the first election in 1952. Congress remained the largest mainstream party and it maintained its dominant role at the Centre under the Indian Parliamentary democracy for a long time. The Socialists were delegated to the middle position.

Political Map Changes

Later in 1967 the Congress party lost seventy-eight seats in the Lok Sabha, retaining a majority of only twenty-three seats. Even more indicative of the Congress setback was its loss of control over six of the sixteen state legislatures that held elections. Though Congress' status as the main party at the centre did not change, the strength of the opposition parties continued to grow at the state level. In Maharashtra the Samyukta Maharashtra movement resulted in a large number of non-Congress representatives being elected to the state legislature. Similar changes also took place in Gujarat. At that time, it appeared that the dominant position of the Congress at the centre was being threatened. During this period Indira Gandhi orchestrated the defeat of Congress party's official candidate to the office of the President of India.

Indira Gandhi did realize that voting pattern was shifting and felt while she was trying to project some radical measures, she must also challenge the established leadership of the Congress and take charge by breaking it. The Parliamentary Board, of which Indira Gandhi was a member, had selected Sanjeeva Reddy as its nominee for the election of the President of India. Indira Gandhi supported V.V.Giri at the last moment. Her pursuit of power and dominating traits led her to take such risks. She came out with the statement, "I would like the Congress members of Rajya Sabha, Lok Sabha and State Legislatures to be allowed to give conscience vote."

She demonstrated her penchant for taking risks again during the Bangladesh war. USA did not want the break up of Pakistan nor did Soviet Union really want to see Pakistan divided. I was in Germany at that time. The leaders of the Social Democratic Party of Germany also suggested that a solution to the conflict in the sub-continent should be found out within the framework of united Pakistan. That was the general opinion of the international community. Despite that Indira Gandhi took a calculated risk. If the Bangladesh coup had failed, Mujibur Rahman would have been killed. Pakistani Army had already killed 80 per cent of the population. The situation was horrible. Her gamble in Bangladesh succeeded.

I will give an interesting account of the machinations during this period. I.K. Gujral narrated this to me. While he was campaigning for Indira's candidature, they were collecting signatures from inside the Congress. Each signature was assigned a serial number. When the serial number reached 40 he had came to the was end of the page. The next page began with the number 61. He remembered sitting in the restaurant of the Western Court. The inflated number was shown to the M.Ps. present in Western Court. They were told that Indira Gandhi had already secured the support of over half the number of Congress members of the Parliament. By manipulating numbers a little jolt was given to the system. Indira Gandhi managed to maintain her supremacy and crush the dissidence within her party.

After the defeat of the official candidate for the office of the president, the Congress party expelled Indira Gandhi. The Congress party split into two, the new factions being the Congress (O), led by Morarji Desai and the other Congress (R) led by Indira Gandhi. To counter the threat of Congress (O), Indira Gandhi ordered parliamentary elections and travelled throughout the country campaigning on the slogan "*garibi hatao*." The Congress (R) won a dramatic victory. In the 1971 elections for the Lok Sabha, the Congress (R) garnered 44 percent of the votes, earning 352 seats. The Congress (O) won only sixteen seats and 10 percent of the votes.

The next year, after leading India to victory over Pakistan in the war for Bangladesh's independence, Indira Gandhi and the Congress (R) further consolidated their control over the country by winning fourteen of sixteen state assembly elections and victories in 70 percent of all seats contested. Her faction emerged as the real Congress and the rebel faction Congress (O) was delegated to a marginal role. Congress (R) assumed the mantle of the main party in the Indian political arena.

Now the question that comes to one's mind is how did this one-party domination end? After 1971, a number of episodes took place, which for the first time started raising doubts about Indira Gandhi's political integrity and capacity to rule. One after another, the License scandal, the Nagarwala scandal, Antulay issue, etc. led to the decline of her credibility and as a result there was rise in support for the Opposition. Though the opposition parties did not gain strength inside Lok Sabha, their campaign against the misrule of the Congress party was striking a cord amongst the masses.

In course of time, Jayaprakash Narayan realized that Indira Gandhi was going in the wrong direction. He gave a call for Total Revolution and set on a whirlwind tour of the country. To give an idea of the impact of JP's campaign had on the masses, I would like to narrate an interesting episode. Whenever JP came to Bombay (after his retirement in politics) the veteran Gandhian Usha Mehta would call me and request me to bring a few people. It would not look good if only 40 or 50 people turned up. I should also come because he was my former leader. His lectures at that time were focused on Bhoodan (donating land). Though he was isolated from mainstream political life, he had retained his stature as a senior statesman. Subsequently, when he started his campaign against corruption in Bihar it was popularly called the JP movement. Between 1971 and 1973 he travelled throughout the country, talking about issues such as freedom, eradication of corruption, and electoral reforms. He attracted a large audience. It was a memorable period. In Punjab there was a large turnout in his meetings and many people said that even during the freedom struggle nobody, including Gandhi, have addressed such mammoth gatherings. The Intelligence agencies gave reported to Indira Gandhi, that JP was getting tremendous support everywhere and that if his movement was not curbed, he would not stop at only processions, but would start civil disobedience.

Fast for Gujarat Elections

Around this time, Morarji Desai declared that he was going to observe indefinite fast to demand fresh elections in Gujarat. In response, Indira Gandhi rushed to the Lok Sabha and declared, "We will not yield to pressure. No, no, we will not hold elections." After a few days she received Intelligence reports that indicated that Morarjibhai's condition was worsening. Even then she did not yield. Morarji was a dogged man. His pulse was slowing down and Intelligence reports said that he might die and that he was not amenable to any pressure.

Then, one day at 4 pm, Indira Gandhi came running to the House. She said, "Mr. Speaker, Sir, I have come to make one important announcement. Though we differ with Morarjibhai Desai, we all have great respect for him. We want him to survive and, therefore, I have come to give an assurance that we will hold the elections in Gujarat; and in consultation with all Opposition Parties we will finalize the date." There was big applause. I just got up and in a lighter vein said, "Madam, the last time you came to the House, you said, 'No, no, no.' But we knew that when a woman says 'no and no,' somewhere in her heart, the answer is 'yes.' She started laughing. This was probably the first time that Indira Gandhi found her authority being challenged by the moral authority of Morarji Desai and Jayaprakash Narayan.

The elections were announced and the members of the Opposition parties formed a political alliance, which was called 'Janata Morcha'. All the candidates fought together on their respective symbols – we, the Socialists, Jan Sangh and Congress (O) fought on our own symbol. We formed the first Janata Government in Gujarat. It was a shock for her. At the State level in Bihar also they had to succumb to the popular sentiment against the Congress party. All over the country JP was attracting crowds. Indira Gandhi feared that if JP was receiving such a support all over the country, a civil disobedience movement would make matters worse for her.

Anyway Indira Gandhi was frightened at that time. In the meanwhile a judge of the Allahabad High Court invalidated her election from Rai Bareli. She approached the Supreme Court, and got a temporary relief on June 24, 1975. The Supreme Court ruled that Indira Gandhi's powers and privileges, as Prime Minister would be unaffected during her appeal against the Allahabad High Court judgment. She decided to act right away. She announced the Emergency on June 25, 1975 and put all her political opponents in prison.

Post-Emergency Elections

Post-Emergency elections were a turning point in the history of Indian democracy. It would be interesting to narrate some of the backroom deliberations before the Opposition parties decided to fight the elections together. I want to refer to my colleague George Fernandes. At that time our party had not merged into the Janata party. The National Executive meeting of the Socialist party was being held. George Fernandes sent a letter to the members outlining his position on fighting the elections. He said, "My advice to the National Executive of the Socialist Party is that we should not contest these elections. We have no time to organize; we have no money. She (Indira Gandhi) will do tremendous organization, and raise a lot of funds. She will defeat the opposition unity and she will legitimize the Emergency and send us back to jail." The National Executive Committee felt that this position outlined by George was totally wrong. Morarji Desai also told his party that he differed with the assessment made by George. Against this background, I prepared a letter to the President of the Socialist Party, took it to George for his signature. The letter stated, "After discussing it with many colleagues, I have come to the conclusion that it would not be proper to boycott the elections and I would urge all to fight with all their might and drown Mrs. Gandhi's Emergency rule." In a way it was her suicidal steps in declaring Emergency that strengthened the position of the Opposition parties in India.

Let us understand, if Indira Gandhi had taken a very sober stand as Jawaharlal Nehru and others used to take, the situation would not have been precipitated and the position of the Congress party as the monolithic political party would not have been compromised.

I strongly feel that the Indian electorate is more mature than we imagine. When Indira Gandhi misbehaved, she was thrown out and when we misbehaved, we were thrown out. Even Jawaharlal Nehru never got as many seats as Janata party did in 1977. So, our follies compounded the follies of Indira Gandhi and as a result of that, she bounced back with a resounding mandate. The Janata Party, which had briefly displaced Congress as the major political party in India, was dislodged from this position and Indira Gandhi brought the Congress party back to the centre stage of Indian politics.

24

Miscellaneous Issues

Committed Bureaucracy

I am a very strong supporter of a process, which Vithalbhai Patel, in the pre-Independence days introduced. He is the architect of the freedom of the Judiciary, separation of the Legislature and the Executive. According to the process he initiated it was decided that officers in Parliament (and Legislatures) should not be drawn from the IAS cadre, who represented the usual executive strata, but there should be a separate legislative cadre. And I have always maintained that if efforts are made to impose IAS officers on the legislature and even when bureaucrats on the legislative panel are available, then the process of separation of Executive and Legislature will be totally destroyed. The process has begun already. Some appointments were made ad hoc. I think that, by and large, the separation of Judiciary, Legislature and Executive has been maintained. We must scrupulously observe this to avoid damage in legislature administration. But all said and done, even a Socialist State and the most liberal organization in power, will need agencies to implement the policies that are decided by the Legislature. I am not among those who are opposed to bureaucrats, but I am opposed to bureaucratism and my experience in the Parliamentary life for five consecutive Lok Sabhas shows that sometimes good measures are defeated by the bureaucratism of the bureaucrats.

Politics cannot be avoided. There has to be socio-economic and political reforms in order to correct the backlog in developmental and social attitudes. This backlog has resulted in uneven distribution of resources and opportunities, which can be corrected only through political action.

I would like to propose an integration of the approaches adopted by some of the stalwarts of Indian politics. Dr Lohia, for example, strived to integrate the concept of Socialism with the scientific attitude of Acharya Narendra Deva. On the other hand, Jayaprakash Narayan's philosophy of Total Revolution, evolved from a multitude of perspectives such as the spirit of social justice reflected in the thinking of social reformers like Mahatma Jyotiba Phule, Dr Ambedkar and Periar (E.V. Ramaswami Naicker), and also from the idea of decentralization and philosophy of humanism to which Mahatma Gandhi was committed. His thinking was also influenced by Kamaladevi Chattopadhyay's ideas on tapping the creativity of the handicraft sector for generating rural employment. JP had great appreciation for Yusuf Meherally's sense of aesthetics and his ethical response to human aspirations and his unwavering faith in secularism. I do believe that India needs a political conviction, which integrates these ideas and ideals.

Social Justice

I would like to give an example of how a political action can change the course of politics. I was a member in the Union Cabinet headed by V.P. Singh and had the opportunity to understand his thinking behind the decision to implement the Mandal Commission report. I firmly believe that despite different assessments about V.P. Singh by some politicians, he performed the historical task of bringing the issue of social justice on the national agenda. Nobody can now dare stage a retreat from this agenda.

Despite the unrest caused after the announcement that the government would implement the Mandal Commission report, the fact remains that social justice issues came to the top of the national agenda and it was established that economics, politics and the problems of social justice must go hand-in-hand. I do share the fear implied in the question that sometimes good economics and good sociology are destroyed by bad politics. Therefore, political action has to be like JP's concept of Total Revolution, which emphasized that Revolution cannot be completed unless all aspects of life are taken into account. JP's concept of Total Revolution includes reconstruction in the economic, social and cultural life of the entire society. The concept of Total Revolution, to my mind, is very relevant today.

Freedom of Press

I would like to address this question within the framework of the role of the press and its relationship with other institutions of democracy. I would like to contextualize that question within the framework of the functioning of the Legislatures and its debates and discussions. At one stage, the Press Council and some other institutions demanded that the privileges of the legislatures should be codified, and legislation be enacted on what constitutes a breach of privilege. That way the press would know the limit to which they can enjoy freedom to report the proceedings of the legislatures. Feroze Gandhi did bring one good measure that whatever was said in the House, could be reported by the press. The question that arose from this was, "What about the danger that the privileged people belonging to the press only would only present their point of view?" The proponents of the proposal to codify the privileges of the Parliament maintained that once the privileges of Parliament are codified, there would be an ambit, and then Press would know what to report and what could not be reported.

However, I foresee a difficulty in codifying the privileges of the Parliament. When the privileges are codified, if one is accused of breach of privilege, he or she can go to the Judiciary and seek justice. Then the proceedings of Parliament or Legislature will come within the ambit of the Judiciary, and thereby annihilate the freedom of the Parliamentary forum. One must understand why the privilege is protected under Article 105 of the Constitution. The freedom available to the common citizens under the Fundamental Rights enumerated in the Constitution is not adequate to pursue certain issues inside Parliament. Therefore, there are certain special rights and privileges given through Article 105 to the Members of

Parliament, so that they have the freedom and legal protection to discuss issues that are of national importance.

While I agree that the freedom of the Press must be retained, I fear that the parliamentary debates would be hampered if privileges were codified. A balance between the rights of Press, the rights of Parliament, and the freedom of Legislature, need to be preserved. It is very important and ultimately it has to be left to the good sense of the Parliament's presiding authorities and also to the responsibility of the media so that a harmonious relationship between the two important institutions of democracy is maintained.

During the Emergency, those who were in power dictated what the Press could write. Much of the information, that needed to reach the readers, did not reach them at all. That was one extreme. On the other extreme were the cases of some members of the Press frivolously casting doubts on Parliamentarians. A positive relationship between the Press and the political institutions will develop only through trial and error and through experience and experiments. Unfortunately, in our country, we still do not have a balance between various wings of our public life. However, I am in favour of that balance. I hope that such a balance will evolve through more education, more propagation of democratic culture and through efforts to foster a liaison between the media and the various wings of administration. This has not happened until now and needs to happen soon.

Right to Strike

Any instrument can be misused. For example, if media is misused and a biased view is presented, the remedy is not muzzling of the media. For instance, take the right of the hungry man to organize agitations. These are real problems, which would not be solved until and unless the poor and hungry are given the freedom to articulate their problems. Only a free Press can provide a voice to the deprived sections of the society. If the Press is banned, problems of the poor, dalits, women etc., would not come before the public and hence there would not be any solution to such problems.

Merely by banning strikes the problems would not be solved. If you try to ban strikes or agitations you end up suppressing the legitimate aspirations as well as the legitimate agitations and then it does greater harm in the long run.

Protection of Environment

As far as environment is concerned, over the past many years, there is an increasing awareness about ecological issues because of the efforts of various NGOs. Irrespective of the government in power, environmental issues have received wide attention. At the same time, for instance, plantation programmes have been taken up in great measure. To my mind, if the Janata government was keen on surviving, we should have pushed through some of the more critical programmes. For instance, the right to work could have been made a fundamental right to be implemented in a phased manner. The implementation could have begun with drought prone and flood prone regions. There was also a need to bring about agricultural reforms. The Centre could strengthen the agricultural sector by giving the farmers incentives.

The Janata Party government in 1977 had given high priority to eradication of poverty. The process of formulating new methods and policies was underway. The defeat of the Janata government left the process incomplete.

Dwindling Standards of Parliamentary Ethics

I have been in the Lok Sabha for five consecutive terms and it was a very hectic period during which I have had the opportunity to work with some of the best Parliamentarians in the history of Indian Parliament. Both the ruling and opposition benches had great speakers and we often had high quality debates. To illustrate the decline in the quality of conduct, I want to go on record about a recent incident that really throws to the winds all the conventions observed by the Speakers and the presiding authorities in the last 50 years of Indian Parliament.

Sometime ago, the Speaker of Lok Sabha, Manohar Joshi released his book titled 'A Speaker's Diary' at a public function. It is written in the Marathi language. Thank God for that, the whole country would not read what he wrote in his book. According to me, there are some objectionable parts in his book, which reflect the charges I am referring to. That is why I want to put my comments on record. I will give an elaborate analysis of why I find certain parts objectionable.

In his introduction, Manohar Joshi writes, "In publishing this Diary, I was inspired by *Speaker's Diary* written by Dada Saheb Mavalankar," (G.V. Mavalankar). There is no comparison between the two books. Mavalankar did not make his diaries public, during his lifetime. His personal diary was handed over to the Parliament Archives a number of years after his death. I may also point out that G.V. Mavlankar's diaries did not have any improprieties, as I will now point out in this case. It is strange that Manohar Joshi has flagrantly violated all norms that have been set for the Speaker's conduct in the Indian Parliament and outside. Right since Vithalbhai Patel's time (at that time he was not called Speaker, he was called President) a number of conventions have been set up for conduct of the Speaker. When he took over as the presiding officer, Vithalbhai Patel announced, "Before taking over this position I was a Member of the Swarajya Party. That was a Parliamentary Wing of the Congress Party but I will no longer associate myself with the party. I will not attend party meetings since as a presiding officer I must not belong to any Party. Only by giving up association with my former party affiliation, can I give impartial rulings."

As you can see from the conduct of Vithalbhai, one of the guiding principles of the conduct of the Speaker in Parliament is that the Speaker does not get involved in the everyday political manoeuvres within the party he formerly belonged to. Now I would like to compare these noble traditions with what Manohar Joshi has written in his Diary. In his book Manohar Joshi has written that he was invited by the Supremo of the Shiv Sena to come to meet him along with Mr. Vikhe Patil, a Minister of State for Finance in the central cabinet. The Shiv Sena chief told the Speaker on the phone that he was going to remove Vikhe Patil from the Cabinet. Then he writes, "That day, he did not come. So, again next day, we discussed but unfortunately I could not prevent his exit from the Cabinet." Now all these manipulations of power politics are not the jurisdiction of the Speaker. In fact, to maintain the dignity of the position of the Speaker, he should not have gone to meet the former party chief. To further substantiate my point I would like to narrate an episode from the past. Once Jawaharlal wrote a letter to Speaker Dada Saheb Mavalankar that he wanted to discuss some urgent issue with him and asked the Speaker to visit Nehru in the Prime Minister's chamber. Speaker Mavalankar returned Nehru's letter with his comments scribbled on the letter that according to the accepted conventions and norms, the Speaker does not go to the Chamber of any Executive, including that of the Prime Minister. He told Nehru that he was free to visit the Speaker in the Speaker's chamber. Jawaharlal Nehru recognized the impropriety in his action and expressed his regrets for sending the letter and followed up with a visit to the Speaker's chamber. Both Nehru and Mavalankar upheld the dignity of the office of the Speaker by their conduct. They were always scrupulous about maintaining norms and conventions.

Jawaharlal Nehru had a taller stature in the Congress party and in parliamentary life than Mavalankar. However, once elected the Speaker, Mavalankar never bowed before the authority in his own Party. Another interesting episode further illustrates the conventions relating to the supremacy of the Speaker over the Prime Minister in the House.

There is a rule in our Parliamentary procedure that a Minister can make a written statement only once in a day. Before lunch, Jawaharlal Nehru made one statement in Lok Sabha and in the afternoon again he got up and said, "Sir, I want to make another statement." Mavalankar replied, "According to the rules, you cannot make two statements on the same day." Nehru started arguing. The Speaker said, "Order, Order, Mr. Prime Minister, take your seat." Mr. Mavalankar never bowed down before the Prime Minister.

In his Diary, Joshi has graphically described what transpired at the in-camera meeting with leaders of the Opposition convened by him to discuss the Iraq War. I think, no Speaker has ever disclosed details of such meetings in the past. In his Diary Joshi has also said that he had made certain recommendations about awarding Padmashree and other awards to two of his party workers. This is a stunning admission by a Speaker of his continued involvement in party affairs.

Then there is a reference to Uddhav Thakre and Raj Thakre and Joshi's meeting with them. He has also mentioned that he had told the Shiv Sena Supremo that they should be restrained.

We have noble traditions of parliamentary conduct set by veterans such as Vithalbhai Patel (in his position as the President of the House), G.S. Dhillon or G.V. Mavalankar (as Speakers). It is extremely important that those who occupy the chair once occupied by these veterans continue to uphold the dignity of the great institution of Parliamentary democracy by adhering to these noble traditions.

I will refer to two-three incidents that exemplify these noble traditions. The first incident relates to the introduction of the Public Safety Bills in the Central Legislative Assembly in 1929. As you might be aware, there was widespread resentment against this bill, because it was perceived as a tool against the freedom fighters. When votes were counted for the admission of the Public Safety Bill No. 1 there was a tie. The President of the Central Legislative Assembly, Vithalbhai Patel, put his casting vote. He could not put his ordinary vote as a Member, but casting vote by a presiding authority was permissible. As a result of his vote, the Public Bill No. 1 was defeated.

Then Public Safety Bill No. 2 was brought for discussion. Vithalbhai Patel got up and addressed the House. He was candid in expressing his opinion that the Public Safety Bill was a derogatory measure to deal with radical patriots, freedom fighters, and to curtail their liberties, to give suppressive powers to the government. He pointed out that while the House was discussing the Public Safety Bill, the Meerut Conspiracy Case was in progress in the court and some of the revolutionaries were being tried. In the Meerut Conspiracy case, he argued, the same issues of patriotism and civil liberties were involved, which were being covered by the Public Safety Bill. Vithalbhai Patel got up and said, "One salient feature of a Parliamentary debate has to be, that no matter which is sub judice, can be discussed in the House. So either government should withdraw those cases in the Meerut Conspiracy Case or I will suspend this debate on Public Safety Bill, as long as the Meerut Conspiracy Case is going on. I will not allow a sub judice matter to be discussed in the House." The next day, when the Viceroy addressed the Central Legislative Assembly to proclaim the enactment of the bill, Vithalbhai expressed his dissent and made a strong reference in the Assembly. As you might be aware, on April 8, 1928 just as Vithalbhai was about to pronounce his ruling on the validity of this draconian legislative measure, Bhagat Singh and Batukeshwar Dutt threw a bomb in the Chamber. It did not kill anyone but produced a big noise and smoke. The point is, Vithalbhai, exercised his position as the president of the Central Legislative Assembly to uphold the sovereignty of the parliamentary and judiciary systems, without fear of antagonizing the British government.

Another historical contribution of Vithalbhai Patel is that he established an independent cadre of the officers of the Parliament. Prior to his decision, officers of the Indian Civil Services (ICS) and later of the Indian Administrative Services (IAS) would be assigned to serve the Legislature. Vithalbhai realized the need to create an independent cadre for the legislature. He introduced the concept of separation of Executive from Legislature. There is another interesting story relating to Vithalbhai asserting the authority of the legislature over the executive within the premises of the Central Legislative Assembly.

This happened the day the House met after the episode involving Bhagat Singh and Batukeshwar Dutt. Vithalbhai Patel was in the Chair. He looked up at the visitors' gallery. He saw an Englishman in policeman's uniform sitting in the Visitors' Gallery. According to the rules, the Speaker is the custodian of the entire House including the Visitors' Gallery. Vithhalbhai looked at the Police officer and said, "Why do I find a policeman in uniform, who does not belong to the Parliament security sitting in the public gallery? With whose permission has he come, only I have the authority to grant permission for placing a security person in the gallery." An Englishman who was the Home Member (at that time a home minister was called home member) got up and said, "Sir, he is sitting here with my permission." Vithalbhai Patel raised his voice and said firmly, "Hold your tongue Mr. Minister and restrain yourself, otherwise I will have to send you out of the House". He had the courage and conviction to maintain the authority and the dignity of his position.

Here is another example of the Speaker of Lok Sabha upholding rules and traditions. When I was a member of Lok Sabha, I had filed a Motion demanding the removal of Justice Ramaswamy of the Supreme Court for alleged corrupt practices, under Article 124(4). 107 Members supported my motion. The Speaker of Lok Sabha admitted the motion. Before announcing his ruling, he set up a Three-Man Committee, three Judicial Members from different States. The committee recommended that the motion be admitted. The motion came up for discussion in the next Lok Sabha. I was no longer a member of the Lok Sabha when the motion came up. I was sitting in the Visitors' Gallery. Some Members pointed out, "This Motion was submitted by Madhu Dandavate in the previous Lok Sabha. But he is no longer a Member of this House. Hence the motion cannot be taken up." The Speaker ruled that according to the rules, once the motion is admitted and reviewed by a Committee, the motion does survive.

Privileges of Parliament

Another parliamentary convention, which Speaker Mavalankar upheld, was pertaining to the privileges of the Members of Parliament. During Jawaharlal Nehru's Prime Ministership, Rajya Sabha had adopted the Special Marriage Bill. N.C. Chatterjee, who was a Member of Lok Sabha, protested strongly against the passage of the bill at a public meeting. Referring to the members of Rajya Sabha he said, "A pack of urchins has passed the Special Marriage Bill." His comments were widely published in the newspapers the next morning. Jawaharlal Nehru and others were extremely agitated by these comments. In response a Privilege Motion was moved against N.C Chatterjee in Rajya Sabha.Unfortunately for the government, N.C. Chatterjee was a Member of Lok Sabha. He was a very articulate member of the House and well versed with the rules governing members' privileges. The moment he found that a Privilege Motion was brought in Rajya Sabha and the papers were sent to Lok Sabha Secretary, he moved a counter Privilege Motion, saying, "Though I am a Member of Lok Sabha, I am being subjected to the jurisdiction of the other House; two Houses are independent. The other House has no right to move a Privilege Motion against me."

Speaker's Forthrightness

In response to N.C. Chatterjee's Privilege Motion, the Speaker Mavalankar got up and announced (after 12 o'clock), "I have a counter Privilege Motion by N.C. Chatterjee." Jawaharlal Nehru was furious. Speaker Mavalankar gave a firm reply to Prime Minister Nehru, "Mr. Prime Minister, please take your seat. So long as I am the Speaker of this House, I will never allow a Member of my House to be subjected to the jurisdiction of the other House. It is irregular." Later a meeting of all the presiding officers of the states and central legislatures was held and there it was unanimously decided that whenever a notice of breach of Privilege comes, it should be transferred to the concerned House and that the Speaker may deal with it, as if it is their own Privilege Motion. That new tradition was introduced. Now this issue received attention because the Speaker Mavalankar took a firm attitude despite opposition from Jawaharlal Nehru.

I want to give another example of a Speaker's forthrightness, which, unfortunately ended on a sad note. In the Fifth Lok Sabha for three weeks we discussed the famous Import Licence Scandal that took place when L.N. Mishra was the Foreign Trade Minister. The government did not yield. We made certain allegations. We had inside information that government knew the facts. Some of us demanded that certain papers that were in government's possession be laid on the table of the House. Then Parliament remained paralyzed for a long time. G.S. Dhillon, who was a great Speaker, gave a ruling, "I suggest that leaders of major political parties should come to my Chamber and the Minister should bring the confidential files about this episode and allow the leaders of all the parties to examine the files." The Opposition accepted the ruling. When G.S. Dhillon had given a ruling from the Chair, the government could not disobey. The meeting was held and the cat came out of the bag. The papers clearly indicated who was guilty. Unfortunately, within a few days L.N. Mishra was killed in a bomb blast at Samastipur in Bihar. The circumstances under which he died raise a lot of doubts. The point is, this was another precedent the Speaker created in order to ensure smooth functioning of the House.

Later, when I became a Minister in the Sixth Lok Sabha, as a courtesy visit, I went to G.S. Dhillon's house and he told me, "Prof. Dandavate, you are doing quite well as a Minister also. In Opposition too you were effective. But I may tell you the government did not take my ruling quite tolerantly. A word was sent to me that I should step down from Speakership. I was offered a ministership with the Transport portfolio." Mr. Dhillon stepped down during the Emergency and B.R. Bhagat became the Speaker. We called him 'Emergency Speaker' later. Dhillon's ruling cost him his position and L.N. Mishra his life. However the truth prevailed.

Mundhra Scandal

I want to narrate another event that has made history in the Parliament. Feroze Gandhi was the first person to raise the Mundhra Scandal in the Parliament. It was widely reported in the newspapers that one Mr.Haridas Mundhra, a businessman sold fraudulent shares to the LIC. Using that information, Feroze Gandhi brought this to the attention of the Lok Sabha. One member of the ruling party said, "You are basing your allegations just on newspaper reports. This is not proper. Do you have evidence?" Feroze Gandhi put his hand in his pocket and said, "Mr. Speaker, Sir, friends of mine want evidence. If you are willing to allow me to lay on the Table of the House the confidential correspondence between the Finance Minister and the Finance Secretary regarding this episode, I am prepared to do it." Some MPs asked, "From where did you get the documents?" Feroze Gandhi said, "I am not a fool to reveal my source, otherwise I cannot fight corruption." The Speaker, M. Ananthasayanam Ayyangar, will be remembered for all times to come by all those who want to fight corruption, because of the ruling he gave. He said, "So long as Hon'ble Member is prepared to take full responsibility for the authenticity of the confidential documents he is seeking to lay on the Table of the House even if they are brought by stealth, I will allow them to be laid on the Table of the House. Mr. Gandhi, you can lay them on the Table of the House." Feroze Gandhi laid the documents on the Table of the House. Then Jawaharlal Nehru had to appoint the one-man Chagla Commission and ultimately it was found out that Mundhra was guilty as charged. So Mundhra was sentenced and T.T. Krishnamachari, the Finance Minister, resigned.

Since the time this landmark ruling was delivered by M. Ananthasayanam Ayyangar, many of the alert members of the Parliament have used it as a precedent. Whenever we gained access to confidential information that was deliberately being hidden from the public eye, we were able to present it to the Parliament without fear of being forced to disclose the source. The veteran parliamentarian Jyotirmoy Bosu once got up and said to the Speaker, "Sir, has the government received the interim Wanchoo Commission Report on Taxation? There is one chapter on Black Money." The members of the treasury benches maintained a studied silence. Jyotirmoy Bosu wanted to force a discussion on certain observations made in the Wanchoo Committee report on black money transactions in India. Since the government refused to acknowledge existence of such a chapter, Jyotirmoy Bosu asserted, "Mr. Speaker Sir, if the government is not producing the report before the Parliament, I have it in my briefcase. Allow me to lay it on the Table of the House." The Speaker allowed Jyotirmoy Bosu to place the report on the Table of the House.

There have been many such instances where Ananthasayanam Ayyangar's ruling helped us place certain documents in Parliament without disclosing the source. H.V. Kamath was allowed to place a CBI Report on the Table of the House using the same precedent, so was I able to place many documents that surfaced during the Bofors controversy.

Splits harmed Socialist Movement

It is unfortunate that the history of the Socialist movement and of the Socialist Party are replete with repeated splits. I want to make it very clear that I was always of a very firm opinion that though there were some differences, it is only a united socialist movement that could provide an alternative to the establishment. I would like to narrate an event that has left a lasting impact on my mind.

The Labour Party's Prime Minister James Callaghan was on a visit to India. Committed to socialist ideas, we invited him to have discussions with the party workers at our party office in Bombay. He replied to various questions and very candidly told us, "We have avoided one blunder in our Socialist movement and the Labour movement in England. Even if we had sharp differences amongst ourselves, we did not split the Party. That is how we have been able to project a clear picture of two alternatives. When the Conservative Party is in power there is a strong Opposition in Labour Party. If change takes place, then the Labour Party takes over and the Conservative Party is in the Opposition. That was possible despite differences on a number of issues." He said on the question of European Market there were differences in the Labour Party, but the differences did not precipitate any split and break-up of the Party.

I am among a few in the socialist movement in India who believe that we may differ, but we should not allow those differences to break the very instrument with which we want to establish a Socialist society. Prem Bhasin, Surendra Mohan, Hem Barua from Assam, Nath Pai, N.G. Goray, S.M. Joshi and others have never been a part of a split either, right from the first split up to the recent one, even when we had joined the Janata Party. At one stage S.M. did leave the party but he took a lead in recommending reunification. He admitted that the split was a mistake.

I will now give you a quick overview of various splits in the socialist movement. In 1953 Asoka Mehta had initiated a theory in the Party about, 'political compulsions of backward economy.' On the basis of this theory he pleaded for the Congress-PSP consolidation. JP had made it clear that though he did not agree with Asoka Mehta's theory, he was not opposed to talks with the Congress when Jawaharlal Nehru had invited the PSP for the talks. The issue was bitterly discussed in the PSP Conference held between 14th to 18th June, 1953 at Betul in Madhya Pradesh. A Policy Commission was appointed and the policy proposal was later accepted unanimously at the Allahabad Conference of the PSP in 1954. However, a new crisis faced the socialists when Pattom Thanu Pillai of PSP was the Chief Minister of Kerala. Violence that broke out in several parts of the Kanyakumari district ended up in police firing killing seven persons. Dr Lohia demanded the Ministry's resignation. However, the National Executive Party while extending an apology to the nation through its resolution decided to appoint an Inquiry Commission to investigate the firing. Dr Lohia and his colleagues insisted on simultaneous resignation of the Ministry even prior to the enquiry. These differences ignited discontent among the followers of accentuating the atmosphere of split.

The situation was accentuated after the adoption of a resolution on Socialism at the Avadi session of the Congress in 1955. After this there were a chain of disciplinary actions. Ultimately the Socialists were split into Praja Socialist Party and Socialist Party led by Dr Lohia in 1956.

After following a lonely path, the Socialist Party later on adopted a policy of not pursuing any alliances with any other party at the level of elections and struggles. The Praja Socialist Party resolved to pursue an opposite course by following the policy of alliances in elections and in struggles. Asoka Mehta's joining the Planning Commission and accepting the membership of a delegation to the United Nations led to the termination of his membership of the PSP.

The next unfortunate event was the joint conference of the SSP consisting of the PSP and Socialist Party to formally launch the Samyukta Socialist Party at Varanasi. Unfortunately due to mutual recriminations and disturbances, it was decided to revive the PSP and ultimately two separate Socialist Parties, PSP and SSP came into being. After going through this circuitous path, after the 1971 elections to Lok Sabha the PSP and the SSP merged to announce a unified party with the name 'Socialist Party' with Karpoori Thakur as President and I as General Secretary.

Here I would like to narrate how sometimes non-issues become the issues of splits. The next issue that arose at the National Executive of the Socialist Party was whether one, who was defeated in direct elections, should enter the Legislature by the backdoor even after a defeat. In fact, I am told that Dr Lohia was opposed to such practice. This issue came up for discussion when Raj Narain was defeated in the direct elections but he had a strong desire to go to Rajya Sabha. So Madhu Limaye, his old colleague, moved a resolution in Delhi, proposing that no one, who is defeated in the direct election, should contest indirect elections. That resolution was passed with a majority vote. It was an indirect hint to Raj Narain to leave the Party. Then Raj Narain collaborated with Chaudhari Charan Singh and Piloo Mody's Swatantra Party - together they formed the Bhartiya Lok Dal and managed to get a symbol assigned by the Election Commission.

When the Emergency was promulgated in 1975, all of us from the socialist movement were imprisoned together. After emerging from the jail, JP insisted that if the Congress were to be defeated, we must have total mobilization of votes. Mere adjustments with parties would not work and therefore, he suggested that we all must form one party. The Janata Party was formed in 1977.

After the Janata Party was formed, again some differences came up. Unfortunately, some of our colleagues from the socialist movement were party to supporting the No-Confidence Motion.

Charan Singh formed the government and Indira Gandhi promised him support after his written request. The day he was to take Vote of Confidence, she withdrew her support and Charan Singh's government was defeated. Then Charan Singh formed the Janata Party (Secular) which later split into Janata Party (A), Janata Party (B) and Janata Party (C), which were later designated as Lok Dal (A), Lok Dal (B) and Lok Dal (C).

Through all these splits, some of us, whose names I have mentioned, remained with the original party. We did not split because I believed what James Callaghan; the former Prime Minister had told us long ago, "If you want to be an alternative focus for power, you cannot afford to go on splitting up the party."

Right from the formation of the Socialist Party up to the latest split when the Janata Dal (S) was named after Janata Dal (U) decided to join the National Democratic Alliance, I did not contribute to the splitting process. On the other hand, George

Fernandes has acquired mastery and finesse in the art of splitting. I have always believed, "Breaking the party is not a way of sorting out ideological and policy differences." The splits have cost us very heavily. The Socialist movement, which was gaining ground in the pre- and post-independence era, got a rude shock as a result of repeated splits. I want to repeat, whatever be the cost, I remained with the original party and did not contribute at all to the splitting process.

Most of the splits were caused due to the temperamental incompatibility between leaders. Of course, some of the splits were motivated by the quest for power. Splitting the party to somehow gain power, points to the demise of idealism in political life.

As I look back

My colleagues, particularly, in the Socialist movement and in Janata movement, decided to felicitate me and donated a purse of rupees 25 lakhs. At that time I had expressed my views that throughout my public life I have held a firm conviction that funds collected from the people must not be used for one's personal life, but only for public causes. I believe that the money earned without my own physical or intellectual labour cannot be claimed by me. This belief emanated from my socialist idealism. I also believe that my decision is consistent with the concept of detachment. I told those who were facilitating me, "Throughout my public life I have moved from door to door carrying a begging bowl to collect funds for public institutions, social causes and political work. I have always felt I was a seeker of financial support for public causes. Now, I feel I am in a position to give. I have now converted myself from being a seeker to a giver." While giving away the money collected for me, I specified that the money be used to support people who fight for justice, and it should be used to nurture sensitivity for culture and human values amongst those who fight for justice. I returned the money donated to me so that it can be used to support those who are involved in constructive activities, struggle against injustice, organizational work, training programmes and work for social change.

I told my colleagues on the occasion, when I ask myself a question as to what are the basic premises of my public life, I find the answer in the experiences of my life. In my public life I keep my one hand on the pages of books that impart knowledge and enlightenment to me, and my other hand is on the hearts of my colleagues engaged in struggles for justice so as to get a feel of their emotions. It is my abiding faith that only a proper balance between deep knowledge and empathy for people's emotions can be a real guide to our thoughts and actions. It is important to complement ideological commitment, dedication and determination with appreciation for music, art, literature, dance and drama, so that one can develop sensitivity to the tender moments of life. My ideas and beliefs were formed through the crucible of struggle, the wedge hammer of constructive work, and through pursuit of knowledge. Close association with great personalities as well as humble devoted party workers at the grass-roots level had a great impact on me.

I would like to recall various ideas that influenced me at different points in my life. I read Marx too early in my life. I was late in reading Gandhi. It was much later that I had the time and opportunity to study and imbibe the ideas of humanists like Phule, Ambedkar and Buddha. As a result, for a while there was an element of dogmatism and imbalance in my thoughts and actions. But as I made a deep study of the writings of these great men, the imbalances and distortions in my thinking were corrected.

I have learned a lot from the stalwarts of the Socialist movement. The erudition and nobility of Acharya Narendra Deva, JP's life of struggle and supreme sacrifice and Dr Lohia's new thrust to Socialist thinking gave a new direction to my thoughts and actions. I had high regard for the sublime character of S.M. Joshi's public life. N.G. Goray's rationalism, concern for social equality and urge for action had a deep impact on me. Yusuf Meherally, whose life symbolized the purity and transparency of a dewdrop on a tender flower, fascinated me. Sane Guruji, who in his thinking, combined father's protective shield as well as mother's compassion, shaped my sensitivities to other people's feelings; my dear friend Nath Pai, who, through his eloquent speeches, gave a melodious voice to human pain, inspired me. In fact, Nath's dream of Konkan Railway became the central point of my action plan for my constituency. My heart overflows with joy when I find that we have been able to accomplish Nath Pai's dream of Konkan Railway.

I deem it a great privilege to have been a Member of Parliament in five consecutive terms in the footsteps of my colleague, Nath Pai, who was in Parliament for three consecutive terms earlier. I deem it a great opportunity to see some of the towering men in Parliament irrespective of their political affiliations.

I am so proud that I was in the Parliament at a time when Indrajit Gupta of the Communist Party was a member. He was a very sharp speaker; every speech of his was well argued. He had the background of the movement. Without getting rattled, with a sarcastic tone, he would drive home the point and he was always heard with rapt attention inside the House. I had personal contact with him. It was one of the memorable associations that I had with him.

Similarly, Jyotirmoy Bosu of CPI (M) was one of the few articulate Members of the Parliament. He was always charged and surcharged by every burning issue, was prepared and would not talk without strong content. Even his most severe critics always used to say, "Very few could equal his promptness, study and his Parliamentary performance".

I had the opportunity to be in the company of men like Atal Bihari Vajpayee and Hiren Mukherjee in the Opposition. Hiren Mukherjee's flair for the English language and literary style was remarkable. I only regret that I entered Parliament after Nath Pai's death and hence could not share his company in the House.

H.V. Kamath's was known for his promptness and wit; I can never forget his performance in the House. He was the old Member of the Constituent Assembly and I often referred to his debates of the Constituency Assembly. Somnath Chatterjee also is a great Parliamentarian.

Above all, the scintillating performance of Madhu Limaye and his deep knowledge of parliamentary procedures and constitutional issues always thrilled me.

Reply with Humour

In my Parliamentary life, I have learned that even if someone tries to have a dig at you in Parliament, it is better to respond with a humorous repertoire rather than get angry. I also realized that speeches made with thorough study and combined with a touch of humour and punch has more impact while facing stiff opposition. Once while I was presenting my budget, my spectacles fell down. A Member from the Congress Benches got up. He said, "Prof. Dandavate, shall I offer you my spectacles?" I said, "No it won't do because it must be shortsighted."

Another incident that comes to my mind is when K.K. Tiwari from the Congress Benches pointingly said I was talking like a CIA Agent. The Speaker and the Congress Members asked him to withdraw his words. My immediate response to his accusations was, "No Sir, let him not withdraw, let it remain on the record so that the electorate should know what language he is using against his critics." However, he was asked to withdraw his comments.

Piloo Mody was known for a great sense of humour. When he was in Rajya Sabha, a lady member from the Congress Party was sitting behind him and he turned around to speak to her while his back was towards the Chair. A member of Rajya Sabha got up and said, "Mr. Chairman, Mr. Piloo Mody is showing his back to the Chair and insulting the House." Piloo responded, "Sir, he is saying that I am showing my back to the Chair. Look at me, I have nothing like back and front, I am only round." Sometimes a very tense House can be brought to order not by the Speaker's hammer but by humour. Fortunately I have experienced this humour in my senior parliamentarians.

At the beginning of every Lok Sabha session, the speaker invites leaders of parliamentary parties for a meeting of the Business Advisory Committee in his Chamber to discuss the issues to be taken up. When I was in the Parliament, the leaders of Opposition parties followed a convention of meeting informally before the meeting with the Speaker, irrespective of our differences. Opposition Leaders would meet at my residence to discuss the issues to be taken up in the business advisory meeting and to chalk out our combined strategy for the session. For many years I hosted this meeting at my residence. There was greater harmony among the Opposition at that time. I may also suggest that such informal meetings also created a common psychological ground for future alliances (such as the National Front). Communal issues were not the main issues at that time.

Pain in the Heart

As I look back and compare and contrast the spirit and heritage of India's freedom struggle against the present political and social atmosphere, I feel a deep pain somewhere in my heart. I am pained to see the divisive forces, which seek to wreck India's composite culture, plural society, the secularism and federalism of the Indian Constitution. I am pained to see that these divisive forces are openly threatening religious minorities that they should join the mainstream, or else feel free to leave India. Our nation was once partitioned in 1947, now I see that divisive forces have stepped up their effort to partition the minds and hearts of the people of our country with perverse passion. In such a critical period, all the forces of secularism and social change must fight back these divisive forces. The time has come to respond to the warning of a poet who said, "In freedom we have appropriated only the tears. Once again light the torches of our life."

Friends' Good Wishes

Many of my friends have expressed their good wishes that I may live for a hundred years, but in my mind, there is one concern. For all these years, I have travelled far and wide in the discharge of my duties in my public life for social causes. If and when I leave this world, I would like to leave when I am firmly standing erect on my feet and not while lying in distress on my back. When I am in the midst of friends and colleagues involved in delightful conversations punctuated by wit and humour, when I am dreaming of the new India, when my one eye is glittering with tears of joy and the other one sparkling with the tears of sympathy for the poor and oppressed, when I am hearing the melodious tunes of the grand finale of a symphony, nature may pick me up without any hesitation. I will not be rattled and will have no regrets.

In the end I must say that I never lose my courage, but I really feel very unhappy for more than one reason. When I see the type of communal hysteria that has developed throughout the country I feel sad. We have come through the freedom struggle and Socialist movement and we never experienced communal feelings inside or outside the Parliament. People belonging to different religions, whether they are Hindus, Muslims, Christians or Buddhists, have made profound contribution in building this country and its Constitution. When I read the speech of a senior leader of the Vishwa Hindu Parishad, who said, "If I am not allowed to go ahead and reach the site of the Ayodhya Temple, there will be communal riots," I feel very unhappy. I could have understood if he had said, the people will be agitated if he was not allowed to reach Ayodhya. But he used the word 'communal riots'. No politician of high stature should ever speak in that tone.

I feel sad about every democratic instrument. In expressing my opinions I do not want to commit contempt of the House. However, the fact is that the standard of debates in the Parliament has deteriorated. As far as public life is concerned, the very essence of our diverse culture is being destroyed; communal harmony is being threatened. With the new policy of globalization, liberalization, and privatization, we find that factories are closing down. As a result, there is more unemployment, and poverty is growing. The markets of the peasants are getting destroyed because they cannot compete with subsidized agricultural products imported from developed countries.

In this country, we saw the assassination of Gandhi, the Father of the Nation, and now we find the denigration of his memory. That is the supreme tragedy. As I witness the changes around me in my own lifetime, as I reflect over these changes as one who has derived so much inspiration from Mahatma Gandhi, I feel that the current political situation is the biggest tragedy of our nation's life and a betrayal of all that Mahatma Gandhi fought for.

25

Future Course

The future course of my life cannot break its link with the past. I have sustained my zest for life through continued involvement in public life and varied interests and movements. In moments of gloom and agony, enlightened works of philosophers, political and social scientists, economists, socialist thinkers, littérateurs and poets have helped me in preserving my deep interest in life.

My wife Pramila shared with me the values and vision of life. She participated in several political and social movements with her deep commitment to the ideals of gender justice and empowerment of women. For these causes, she fought from the forum of Parliament as well as through struggles outside. Her activism was a great source of support and inspiration to me. In all the successes I achieved in various walks of my personal and public life, Pramila's unstinted support and inspiration had a great share. I deeply feel the void created by her death on January 1, 2002.

In the evening of my life, my quest for truth, justice, freedom and equality will still continue. So will continue my search for aesthetic joy in the works of eminent thinkers and writers in the fields of knowledge, the arts and literature. Though I have undergone more than fifteen minor and major surgeries, I have survived and maintained my optimism with the help of my will power and medical care.

The show must go on.

Time alone will pronounce:

> *Drop the curtain—*
> *the show is over.*

Appendix - 1

The Joint Statement with JP*

"We discussed the political situation in Bihar created by rampant corruption, ruthless repression, abdication by the Legislature of its legislative powers with total reliance on Ordinances, galloping inflation, unemployment and frustration among the youth due to the prevalent educational system, unresponsive to their urges and aspirations.

"Against this background we felt that the demand for the dissolution of the unrepresentative Bihar Assembly and Ministry and emergence of a truly democratic alternative on the basis of free and fair elections must receive priority.

"However, we are convinced that if the peaceful movement in Bihar is to take deeper roots and achieve its objective, vital socio-economic problems of workers, peasants and weaker sections must find adequate reflection in the movement.

"In this context we feel that the struggle of the working class against wage freeze and spiraling of prices and for a need based minimum wage must be strengthened. Similarly, the agricultural labour's and peasants' fight against evictions and for fair wage

---

* The text of the joint statement signed by Jaya Prakash Narayan, P. Sundarayya, Promode Das Gupta (CPI-M) and Madhu Dandavate (Socialist Party) and issued in Patna on September 18, 1974.

and share as also for distribution of surplus and waste lands must be intensified.

"The efforts to combat hoarding and black-marketing and ensure distribution of essential commodities at cheaper prices must be taken up with earnestness.

"We agreed that we shall have frequent consultations among ourselves to radicalize and intensify the movement in Bihar while adhering to our respective ideological stances".

Appendix II
Bofors Payoff - I*

I have carefully listened to the statement by the Defence Minister and more carefully to the intervention by the Prime Minister. The Prime Minister said that neither the Press nor the Opposition has made any specific allegation and if some evidence is brought forward and it drew a fine distinction between the evidence and proof, he will be prepared to go into the matter and have some sort of a probe. Recently, many transactions have taken place and this House has recently discussed the German deal regarding submarines, and today we are having this other deal — the Swedish deal about Bofors. It is regarding the field guns. He very categorically said that he had taken a firm decision that no middleman will be permitted in all these transactions. I would like to draw the attention of this House, and particularly the attention of the Prime Minister, that when one of my colleagues in the discussion the other day mentioned one particular agent and said, "Is this the agent who is involved in that West German deal, it is on record — I have checked the record." the Minister of Defence said, "I neither accept nor deny". My comment to his response was, "You have really followed a non-aligned policy"! This particular affair was announced first on the Swedish State Radio.

---

* Speech delivered by Prof. Madhu Dandavate in Lok Sabha on April,20th, 1987.

First the news item appeared through Reuters as an announcement on the Swedish State Radio, which made a specific allegation that in this particular deal of the field guns, Indian politicians were bribed. The quantum was mentioned and they insist that this particular information was correct. After that, some contradictions came. The contradiction came from the Swedish company, a contradiction also came from the Indian Government. The Swedish State Radio had first made the allegation that bribery and corruption had taken place. The allegation was specifically against the Indian politicians. After the contradictions appeared from Bofors as well as the Government of India, the same night the Swedish State Radio made one more announcement and in the second announcement, after the contradictions by Bofors and by the Government of India, they reiterated the allegation and said, "First, we stand by the allegations that we have made in our earlier announcement. Second, we have the correspondence and the documents at our disposal and at the appropriate time we will be prepared to release them." They say that the correspondence between those who have actually acted as middlemen and the Swiss Bank is also there. We also got the bank code numbers of those in whose accounts the money has been kept. They went on giving further details. They said that the entire amount of bribe was not paid in one installment, but they were paid in four installments. They say "We know the code number and the bank account" and they further said that the code name is "Lotus". That is what the Swedish Radio said.

I am not going into the details about the quality of the field guns, if the range, which was mentioned, is really the actual range of those guns, etc. These are the details, which the Defence Minister will take care of. But what I am concerned about now is also the bonafides of the firm, Bofors. Actually, as far as the Swedish Government is concerned, they have blacklisted certain countries to which arms should not be sent by any company at all and it would clearly appear that this company with which we have the transactions — the deal for field guns — had clandestinely smuggled arms, field guns, into the Middle East and Iran. What are the bonafides of a company with which they have entered into transactions? This I want to highlight, and, therefore, I ask, why was it not questioned that the company, which is smuggling arms to those countries, was blacklisted by the Swedish Government itself? If that company is selling arms to them, why are they trying to deal with such a company when its bonafides are not accepted prima facie? In his statement the Minister of Defence has talked of destabilization. Here I want to tell the House that any exposure of corruption in a democratic country does not lead to the process of destabilization. In a democratic country like Japan the Prime Minister was involved in the Lockheed scandal, the matter was inquired into, but no country said, and India also need not say, that that led or will lead to destabilization. On every occasion we try to expose any scandal here in the House, we are told that our action would lead to destabilization and therefore, I said that destablisation is not the consequence of any eradication of corruption.

Mr. Feroze Gandhi was foremost in exposing the Mundhra scandal. The Sirajjudin affair was discussed in the House. The Defence Minister's jeep scandal was brought before the House. But nobody said in the times of Pandit Jawaharlal Nehru, the first Prime Minister, that the eradication of corruption and the campaign against corruption would ever lead to the destabilization of the country.

In the Fifth Lok Sabha, in close succession, three important corruption episodes came up in this very House. The import licence scandal was there. It was followed by the Nagarwala's State Bank scandal in which Rs.60 lakhs were taken only when somebody spoke on the telephone. "I am Mataji speaking. I want Rs. 60 lakhs", and Rs.60 lakhs were given. All this happened. What is wrong? The Finance Minister could not justify that.

I would like to point out to you that very often through the Press, certain news items have been picked up and on the basis of that, enquiry has taken place. The Fairfax affair was not initially taken up from the floor. In the case of one particular case, the matter came up. Then a contradiction was made by the chairman of the agency. When the matter came up, initially, they said, there was no need to appoint a Comission of Inquiry. Afterwards, actually the Commission of Inquiry was appointed.

My conclusion is, since the Right Hon. Prime Minister had already said that if anything is brought to his notice, and concrete allegations are there, he will be prepared to make an inquiry, I would suggest this — let there be a parliamentary probe. Let them visit Stockholm, meet the authorities and find out the documents and the correspondence thereon. The whole matter can be settled amicably and in the interest of the country.

Bofors Payoff-II*

Despite many manipulations in the past to see that the motion that I had proposed in different forms was sidetracked and discussion evaded, because of the ingenuity of the rules of procedure of the Lok Sabha and also the determination and vigilance of the opposition, and the consideration of the Business Advisory Committee (BAC) followed by the consideration of the House in adopting the BAC's report, I have been able to have this opportunity for discussion on the subject. I rise to initiate the discussion on the announcement by the Chief Public Prosecutor of Sweden regarding inquiry into the alleged bribe paid by Bofors in the Howitzer deal.

It is in the fitness of things that one particular criticism that has been voiced against us in this House and outside, I should take cognizance of. It is a cardinal point that has become extremely crucial in the discussion of the entire subject. After the announcement of the Chief Public Prosecutor of Sweden regarding the inquiry to be taken up on Bofors, a question was posed to the Opposition. Is it in keeping with the dignity of this Parliament and the dignity of this country that we should seek the assistance of an agency outside the country to investigate the matter? As a Member of Parliament, I consider myself accountable to this House. Even a veteran like Prof. Ranga had doubts about our respect for the nation's prestige and our patriotism. I consider myself answerable

---

*Speech delivered by Prof. Madhu Dandavate in Lok Sabha on August, 26, 1987.

to a veteran like Prof. Ranga. In that spirit, I would like to raise certain points.

You may recall that in 1975 Maharani Gayatri Devi had gone to the United States and her diamond jewelry was stolen. Mrs. Indira Gandhi was then the Prime Minister. Mrs. Gayatri Devi lodged a complaint; and with the consent of the Prime Minister, a foreign agency was engaged to detect the theft of the jewelry; and the same foreign agency was asked to go into the assets of Gayatri Devi.

Then there is a statement by Bhure Lal as the Director of the Directorate of Enforcement, before the Thakkar Commission, that he was compelled to hire Fairfax agency because he had no separate agency of investigation abroad. Earlier the Joint Secretary, Ministry of Finance, had gone abroad and reported that no investigation was possible on our own. I would like to point out to you a third important instance.

The appointment of a foreign agency in principle, was approved by the Prime Minister on two or three occasions, when Bhure Lal saw him and when V.P. Singh saw him.

Then, there has been a confession by the Directorate of Enforcement that "we have no means of investigations abroad and therefore we have dropped the German submarine deal investigations". I am trying to put forward an argument, by giving instances, that bringing a foreign agency for a proper purpose is in keeping with the dignity of this country and there is nothing unpatriotic in that.

The details about Ajitabh Bachchan's apartment in Switzerland were found out by a private detective agency in Geneva. I have not made any defamatory remarks. I have only stated a fact that the agency was employed.

Again, when General Vaidya died at Pune, the investigation of the murder was handed over to a foreign agency.

In the Charles Shobhraj case, an international smuggler involved in corruption, Interpol's cooperation was sought for proper investigation.

You will be surprised that as far as the Bofors problem is concerned, I have with me a copy of the Swedish report. The Indian Government requested the Swedish Government to investigate the details about the Bofors episode. And today only the dispatch from Stockholm has confirmed that. Therefore, it is my submission in the context of our welcoming the Chief Public Prosecutor's inquiry in Sweden, that it is perfectly in order, it is consistent with our patriotic intentions and it is consistent with the dignity and honour of the country, in the interest of carrying out the investigations and in the interest of security, it is perfectly in order to utilize any foreign agency. The Stockholm dispatch of August 25 1987 states:

"The Swedish Prime Minister, Ingvar Carisson, has been under strong Indian pressure to investigate allegations that Bofors bribed Indian officials to win the Howitzer gun contract in February, 1986"

I would like to urge that we are more interested in loss to our exchequer and whether bribes are received by Indian officials and politicians or whether they are received by non-Indian relatives either of politicians or officials, we are just not concerned. And, therefore, we will insist that when this enquiry is being conducted in Sweden, let there be no distinction at all, between the Indian officials and their relatives who are non-Indians. We are not concerned. We are concerned about the threat to the nation's security caused by corruption in Defence deals.

The Swedish Foreign Minister, Anderson, has also suggested that a citizens' commission also probing the deal be permitted to scrutinize documents normally kept confidential for State security and business secrecy.

I welcome the statement and I hope in the light of that, without bringing into question matters like business secrecy or the question of the nation's security, other matters will be gone through.

In this very House whenever the question of inquiries were raised and especially when the inquiry is directed towards finding the truth about acts of corruption, and it is sought to be done by some agency outside the country, there has been often a talk of destabilization. I do not want to dwell on this in detail. But I want to remind this House once again about it.

Sir, it is corruption that destroys the democratic fiber of the country and it is corruption that destroys the stability of the country. The fight against corruption never destroys the stability of the State, it never destroys the stability of the system, it never destroys the democratic fibre of the country.

I mentioned in this House that in the famous Lockheed scandal in Japan, the Prime Minister of Japan was involved. It was established that he was responsible for the scandal. But, even then the Japanese system did not become unstable. No less a person than President Nixon was involved in the Watergate Scandal. When the members of his party threatened that he will be subjected to impeachment, they were not accused of contributing to the process of destabilization. Similarly, here, whenever we demand an inquiry into corruption in high places either by an agency inside the country or by an agency outside, it should never be taken as encouragement to the process of destabilization. On the contrary if all corruption scandals are unearthed, the democratic fiber of the Indian democracy will not be destroyed, it will be strengthened. That is our contention.

As far as the probe by the Chief Public Prosecutor of Sweden is concerned, the question is posed that when the parliamentary panel has already been set up, what is the propriety of having such a panel?

The nationals of Sweden can be summoned only by the Swedish Government. That is absolutely clear. When Bofors are involved, just as some persons in India might be involved in the corruption some nationals of Sweden might be too. Some others might also be involved. When our Parliamentary probe goes into the matter, can we bring them to book? Our joint parliamentary committee may go ahead with this work. I wish them good luck. But at the same time, if there are foreign nationals in Sweden who are guilty of collusion with Indian officials, Indian politicians and they are guilty of having perpetrated a fraud, in that case it is very necessary that they should be investigated by an agency which has the right to summon them, which has the right to bring them to book, and they should be within the jurisdiction of the laws of the country in which they might have committed the crime. This is an important aspect.

There is a precedent of pre-trial inquiry about Bofors itself and that is in Singapore. A pre-trial inquiry had taken place and there again, Bofors were involved. Bofors seems to be notorious for international frauds.

As far as the question, why not the parliamentary joint probe and why must we insist that this probe will bring successful results, is concerned, we have made our position absolutely clear. We did not emphasise in our letter to the Prime Minister so much on the chairmanship of the Joint Parliamentary Committee and the composition of the committee, but mainly the powers of the committee. I may repeat when you pose the question to us that, "when the parliamentary probe is already set up, why do we want the Chief Public Prosecutor to go into the problem", we had demanded four important powers for the Parliament Committee.

That committee should have the power to go into all decisions and policies regarding the defence procurement and storage ever since 1980 because we are repeatedly told that the decision was taken in 1980 that there should be no middlemen. And if the decision was taken in 1980, it is a logical corollary that in the context of this they should be examined. There should be the power to summon the ministers. There should be power to go into the German submarine deal.

Lastly, the foreign nationals may or may not come, but this committee should have the power to hear the evidence of those who desire to appear before the Committee.

These are the four minimum terms and powers that we had mentioned. Unfortunately, even in the parliamentary probe there seems to be an impropriety. A member who is likely to be the Chairman of this parliamentary committee was a member of the Cabinet. My suggestion is that while appointing any person as the Chairman of this Committee, he must not be a member of the Cabinet at a time when these decisions regarding defence are being taken.

I would like to say something about two documents. The letter of denial of allegations from Bofors was read before Parliament. And a lot is made out of that. They said that they have not given the commission. They have flatly denied the charges that are being investigated. I would like to point out through you to this House the tradition of Bofors. The Prime Minister had already handed over to us the copy of the Swedish National Audit Bureau report. In that very report they have pointed out that Bofors have already told the National Audit Bureau that no agreement existed regarding the payment of commission and they did not make the payment of commission. After that, the same National Audit Bureau, which investigated the entire matter, came to the conclusion that, on the basis of the evidence, there exists an agreement about the payment of commission by Bofors to.... Only those dots are to be deciphered. So, if the National Audit Bureau could not accept the bona fides of Bofors, I think the Indian Parliament need not be over enthusiastic to accept the bona fides of Bofors only because their letter has been read on the floor of the Parliament. Have we forgotten that even in the House of Commons in U.K. a very prominent personality holding the Defence portfolio had made a statement and for having misled the Parliament, he had to tender his resignation? So, remember that Ministers sometimes have also misled Parliament. It is quite like that Bofors had sent the letter which need not be correct, and I say this on the basis of evidence given by the National Audit Bureau that they themselves rejected the denial of Bofors that they had indulged in the payment of commission.

I would like to refer to another important document, the most counter productive document. The Prime Minister made a statement in this very House and many members welcomed it. He made it clear and said, "I want to make it explicitly clear that I am not at all involved in this Bofors scandal. I am not personally involved, my family members are not involved." So, we respect everybody's words. He has made that statement on the floor of the House. But I feel that it was a very counter productive statement in the sense that he has only clarified about his family, which according to our accepted connotation, would be oneself, one's wife and one's children. That is supposed to be a family. What happens about others close to them? What about the colleagues, what about the officers, what about the politicians and what about the distant relatives? They do not fall into the category of the 'family'!

There are many Members of Parliament cutting across party lines who would feel very much embarrassed by this statement. They say that he has only given a clean certificate to himself and his family but what about other relatives and what about friends and what about those who publicly said in the statement that they have always stood by the Prime Minister?

Sir, I am happy that the New Minister for Defence, K.C. Pant, is here. On 20th April the Defence Minister made a statement. He flatly denied those allegations made on the Swedish Radio regarding commissions, payment of commissions, etc. and all the allied problems. But after that the Swedish National Bureau's Report has clearly established that these problems exist, I think he has tried to mislead the House. Of course, today he will speak again and correct himself. I know K.C. Pant; whenever he commits a mistake he is always prepared to rectify. It is very likely that he will change the statement. Very often there is discussion about the names. Some of our colleagues have asked for the names. At least one name has been discussed all over the world and commonly accepted by members on both the sides of this House. For instance, Chadha's name has been mentioned. Within the framework of what the Prime Minister said, I will take up this issue. As far as Chadha is concerned, the Prime Minister unfortunately tried to misguide the House on Bofors' agreement with Chadha, "Bofors" is not defamatory, "agreement" is not defamatory and "Chadha" is not defamatory. I am referring to the Bofors agreement with Chadha. The Prime Minister and the Government misguided the people. He said, "There were no middlemen at the point of signing the contract". There is reference to the Bofors agreement with Chadha.

The agreement with Chadha was signed on January 3, 1986. The agreement was signed, there is nothing defamatory. The agreement would be valid up to 31st December 1990. So, this particular statement and clarification that is offered by the Prime Minister to my mind appears very misleading.

I have with me an in-house booklet of Greaves Cotton 1985-86. L.M. Thapar is the Chairman of Greaves Cotton — nothing defamatory in that. He is the concessional distributor for Saab-Scania AB, which supplied two trucks for the Bofors 155mm FH77B Howitzer according to this in-house booklet of the Greaves group of companies. The Photostat copy, if he requires, I am prepared to give. I will not give him the original copy. Saab-Scania has been subcontracted by Bofors to manufacture two trucks. Thapar, through his company Greaves Cotton, is the biggest arms dealer. That is nothing defamatory.

According to the company's official book, Greaves Cotton represents 42 Defence manufacturers as their distributors. According to informed sources, over the last 4 years Rs. 14,000 crores worth Defence equipment were bought and 75% of these were transacted through L.M. Thapar. As Chairman of Greaves Cotton, Thapar has direct access to persons in high places.

The CBI was tipped off by the Economic Intelligence Bureau and in the raid on Thapar in March 1987, documents about the Bofors deal were found. I would like them to lay them on the table of the House.

Thapar is the link through whom Bofors pay-offs were paid in Swiss Bank accounts. I would like to know whether that is a statement of fact. It is because this is the news that has appeared in the economic journals. I would like to ascertain that.

The two trucks brought by Bofors from Saab-Scania were over valued by more than Rs.100 crores and the balance of the excess amount was siphoned off by L.M. Thapar. I would like the Minister to make an inquiry into it. Even if he hands it over to the Joint Parliamentary Committee I do not mind.

Now there is an interesting aspect. Thapar was arrested and released on bail, despite his pleading guilty to 15 of the 18 charges made by the Enforcement Directorate. The cases seem to be shelved. I would like to know what are the facts. Since he is connected with the deals with which Bofors is connected, I would like the Minister to go through all these matters and make the necessary statement on the floor of the House.

I would like to say a word about the Bofors delegation. Bofors first refused to reveal the names on the basis of "customer confidentiality"? On June 11, the Nobel Industry, i.e. the parent organization, argued that India is a customer. Therefore where is the question of "customer confidentiality? " On June 27, Bofors argued that those who accepted commission did not want their names to be revealed. Is this to be called "customer confidentiality?"

Those who take the bribes, will they ever tell Bofors, "Yes you can announce from the house tops that we are the guilty and we are the people who have swallowed bribes? " They will never say that. After his return from a foreign tour, the Prime Minister rejected the idea of welcoming a delegation, saying, "We do not want to meet the delegation." When Bofors are saying they are prepared to send a delegation, why is it that the Prime Minister is rejecting a delegation coming to India? Against this background, he draws a very fine and subtle distinction. He said, they need not meet him. They need not meet the Government, but meet the Joint Parliamentary Committee, which will be set up. That is, he tried to explain away the initial lapse. It does not matter. Even if the lapse ultimately is corrected, and the correct position is taken, I have no objection to that.

A word about the credibility of Bofors. What is the nature of this organization with which we have entered into a deal? Forget all the laws about our country. But what about the Swedish laws? What about the Swedish guidelines? As far as the Swedish Government is concerned, they had blacklisted certain countries and warned all the exporters of arms, that arms should not be sent to those blacklisted countries. There was a reference to the Middle East, Iran and South Africa. But to all these blacklisted counties, Bofors were able to send clandestinely all these arms!

In addition, there was some sort of a collusion in France and in that case, which involved France and Singapore, a pre-trial inquiry had already started. That itself shows the type of company with which you are trying to have an arrangement as far as a business deal is concerned.

More than that, I do not want to say anything by which India's security will be harmed. I hope that the guns that have been provided are not sub-standard guns. Of course we have a case where we have a contract with one country regarding guns, and a contract with someone else for ammunition!

Sometimes the complaint is about both. Repeatedly, newspaper reports have appeared that some of the experts in our army and defence forces have said that the ammunition that we are securing for these guns is sub-standard and some journals have said that even the guns are sub-standard. I hope that this is not true.

I do not want to say anything by which our defence forces will be demoralized.

I have only said that I hope that I will be proved wrong. And, therefore, let them go into this problem and let us assure this House that all this news about sub-standard quality is wrong, and as far as the quality of the guns and ammunition is concerned, the Government should assure us that the security and defence of the country are not at all in danger.

All those problems that are placed before you make it explicitly clear that there are skeletons in the cupboard. The Parliamentary probe might be able to expose some of them. The Chief Public Prosecutor from Sweden might be able to discover some. The Citizens Commission might be able to do that. But as far as this country is concerned, you go from one corner to another and whatever you may say on the floor of the Parliament and whatever statement the Prime Minister may issue, as far as the common man is concerned, he feels that there are certain issues which the Government are covering up as far as the Bofors deal is concerned. And that is why the credibility of the Government has been eroded not only on grounds of other issues like communalism, terrorism and unemployment, etc. but even on the question of corruption in high places. This Government must seek the fresh mandate of the people.

Bofors Payoff-III*

Before I come to the various documents, I would like to refer to some very important lapses in this House, which are closely related to the subject under consideration. The documents that are published by The Hindu on the 22nd and 23rd June, 1988, and documents published earlier on 21st April, had created a grave situation.

I wish to draw your attention to the fact that on the 4th July 1988, I submitted to you a notice of privilege against the Prime Minister, the Defence Minister and against Mr. Win Chadha, and I ought to have included some others in the VIP list. I am deliberately starting with this because they are closely related to the subject under consideration and discussion today.

I wish to draw your attention to the fact that on 20th April 1987 the Defence Minister Shri K.C. Pant, made a written statement in this House and assured the House that as far as the Bofors transactions are concerned, there has been no involvement of a middleman and there has been no payment of commission at all. When the debate went up, the Prime Minister intervened. In my notice, from the Lok Sabha records, I have quoted what exactly was said by the Prime Minister, Shri Rajiv Gandhi. He again repeated that there was no question of a middleman and there was no question of any commission or bribe being paid. At a later stage, the Joint Parliamentary Committee was set up to enquire into Bofors. When the Committee investigated all the matters and the

---

*Speech delivered by Prof. Madhu Dandavate in Lok Sabha on July 28, 1988.

report was completed, almost at the same time when the Report was being presented to this House, we had before us the first important dispatch from The Hindu. If I remember right, it was on 22nd April 1988 the banner headlines announced 'Bofors Pitco payments linked to Hindujas — documentary evidence' and the documents were published in that paper.

Mr. Chadha was asked to appear before the committee. I don't want to go into how he came here, whether he imposed any conditions, whether some concessions were given to him, whether an assurance was given to him that certain arrests will not take place, whether it was assured that he will have a safe exit from the country. The irony of the situation is that the very persons who were supposed to be guilty number one and two, were asked to stand in the witness box and they were given VIP treatment. They made certain statements.

In that very Report that has been submitted over here, we have been told as to what exactly was stated by them. It is stated in the Joint Parliamentary Committee Report on Bofors in para 7.159: "During his examination Shri Chadha further affirmed as under: He was never a middleman, or an agent of Bofors in so far as he never performed any functions of a broker or a commission agent and was not engaged in any selling activities."

We have to rely on the Report. Categorically he denied that he has acted as anybody's agent and received commission. As far as Mr. Win Chadha is concerned, the Prime Minister is concerned and the Defence Minister is concerned, two of them are on record in this House and the third one is on record in the Joint Parliamentary Committee. If you accept the authenticity of the documents that appended in The Hindu, very clearly the Prime Minister, the Defence Minister and Mr. Win Chadha had misguided the House deliberately, committed contempt of the House and committed breach of privilege of the House. That is my contention. This House, through this debate, must take a serious note of the breach of privilege committed by the Prime Minister of the country, the Defence Minister of the country and Mr. Win Chadha. Of course, I do not want to put Mr. Win Chadha on the pedestal of the Defence Minister and the Prime Minister, but unfortunately they are linked up together. I mean the breach of privilege. Therefore, this is the most important aspect that has to be taken note of.

The question arises and I am sure that when you inquire into the matter to decide whether there is a prima facie case, I know that your first argument and premise will be whether those documents of The Hindu are reliable and authentic. If they are proved to be reliable and authentic, then these Members have committed a breach of privilege.

Now I will explain as to why I contend that there is an authenticity to these documents. There are two or three aspects. In the past, whenever any of us from the opposition quoted any document that was embarrassing to the ruling party and the Government, there was always the cry of "CIA agent",… "CIA agent".

The question is what is the authenticity, and I have two points to put forward here to establish indirectly the authenticity of these documents. First, in past, whenever documents were quoted or allegations were made, it was said they were fabricated or we are somebody's agents, but this time, strangely enough, when these documents were published, not only members of the ruling party did not say that these are machinations of some agents or CIA agents but they said that they were instituting a CBI inquiry to find out whether there was a prima facie case in the documents that had been published. Probably investigations come later on. But the first thing that the CBI would have decided is whether it is worthwhile going into the material in these documents. If they were to find out at the very outset that the documents are fabricated and they have been engineered, straightaway they would have reported to the government that we need not proceed with the investigations.

Second, in some of the documents that have been published in The Hindu a reference has been made to Win Chadha and it has been stated that there are certain evidences against Win Chadha having acted as an agent and certain payments having been made in certain bank accounts. All those documents are there.

You may recollect when Win Chadha came here to appear before the Joint Parliamentary Committee, at that time when his work was over, he was expected to return to the United States. At that time there were no restrictions. When he came, he got the royal treatment and when he was to go away he would have got similar treatment. There were certain rumours that he was likely to be arrested or his passport likely to be confiscated, but nothing of that type happened. But when the report appeared in The Hindu, the government warned Win Chadha that he could not leave the country at all. Initially they did not tell Win Chadha that he must not leave the country but only when these documents were published in The Hindu in which indictment of Win Chadha was made, then the Government also felt there were some skeletons in the cupboard of Win Chadha. Under those circumstances, they told him that he could not leave the country. On analysis of this indirect evidence, Government did take cognizance of the documents, which were printed in The Hindu. And as a result, he was told not to leave the country. I have got all the documents and I need not go through all of them.

As far as all these documents are concerned, to my mind, four aspects have been fully established. First, despite the denials by the Joint Parliamentary Committee, despite the denials by Mr. Win Chadha and others, it is established on the basis of the authenticity of the documents that secret agreements did exist and they are available here. I need not lay them on the table of the House because they are laid on every table in every house in the country! Second it has been clearly established, that commissions are paid. Third, it has been established that Win Chadha is linked up with Svenska payments. And fourth, it had been clearly established that the story of winding up charges is only a cooked up and a cover-up story. All the documents are there. Some manipulation of the dates is there. I will just make it explicitly clear that there is nothing like winding up charges. Some of the documents, which are there, have made these things explicitly clear. Without quoting all the documents, only I will give the reference. There are important extracts from JPC's report on Bofors, which clearly conflict with whatever has appeared in The Hindu.

I am quoting from the Joint Parliamentary Committee's report:

Bofors had not used any middleman, representative or agent to represent the company with the Indian authorities in order to win the Howitzer contract and negotiations took place directly between the Ministry of Defence and Bofors.

Bofors had never paid or conspired to pay any bribes in connection with the Howitzer contract.

There is no evidence to show that any part of the winding up costs was paid to any Indian resident in India or abroad.

There are non-resident Indians and there are non-Indian residents. There is a reference to both, and further.

"7.159. During his examination, Shri Chadha further affirmed as under:

He was never a middleman or an agent of Bofors in so far as he never performed any functions of a broker or a commission agent and was not engaged in any selling activities."

Now I will only make a reference to the important documents. I do not want to read them. Number one, reference to documents giving evidence of commission. If you look at Frontline, they have just put all together (page 24).

Number two, a wonderful table of coincidences: Svenska and Win Chadha's Anatronic (page 25). A number of coincidences are given here.

The third is a very important reference. The Internal documents of the Swedish Central Bank giving a monthly statement of transactions involving foreign exchange.

"According to the transaction listed 5th on January 10, 1984 a commission payment (coded '62' of SEK 174,522) was made to 'Pitco Co Sangham Ltd."

This is from page 29 of Frontline. A communication from A.E. Services and another document, regarding a single payment by Bofors of SEK 50.46 million as commission to A.E. Services. The commissions have been firmly linked to payments made by the Government of India to Bofors in 1986-87 against invoiced deliveries or as advances. You can find this on page 32. These documents leave no doubt that payment of commission had taken place to the front companies. In this connection, I would like to have an answer to a specific question. A.E. Services is at least an important institution in this entire House of Corruption. There seems to be too many transactions. Just now, that is not the matter under discussion, but it is reliably learnt that as far as the contract of the Westland helicopters are concerned, it is the A.E. Services, which have given the contract. The percentage has been fixed up and all the documents to which I made a cursory reference have been published in The Hindu by Chitra Subramaniam who has worked out all the details, as to what are the details of the contract, what is the amount involved, what is the percentage fixed, what are the signatures, etc. Therefore, all these details having been given, and it is clear that as far as these details are concerned, clear cut payment of commission has taken place and bribes made. Now, therefore, I would like like to know from the Defence Minister that as far as the A.E. Services are concerned, is it a fact that they were given the contract for Westland helicopters, and what was the percentage of commission, which was actually kept?

I would like to know the replies from the Hon. Minister to specific queries. I would expect exact and clear answers. In spite of the information regarding front companies with their account numbers, commissions paid and the amounts of contracts, no successful enquiry could be made. I have gone through the report. They say that some of them were managed only by women. But that does not stop the mischief. I do not want to make any general allegations against women.

Bofors and Win Chadha who were in the dock as culprits were put in the witness box by JPC and their contention was relied upon. Why is it that you rely upon this and especially when these details have come out? No further information was sought from Sweden after the National Audit Bureau had submitted its report, certain names were dropped out or omitted on the basis of commercial confidentiality and because of their commitment to the banks. A news had appeared and a complaint had been made in that country that after all these documents had come up and so many names had been revealed, how was it that the Government of India did not make any reference to Sweden.

A committee in Sweden in enquiring into the Bofors issue; that is called the Constitutional Committee. It is a Committee of the Parliament of Sweden. There has been a pressure from Members of both sides, the Members of the ruling party as well as from the opposition parties. That is the beauty of the Swedish experiment and they are insisting, "Do not try to cover up anyone, let the Constitutional Committee go ahead with thorough investigations." Why is it that we are not at all trying to seek any help from the constitutional committee, which had already completed a lot of its work? Let the Government tell the House whether one of the front companies mentioned in the documents was the company to which, as I said earlier, the Westland Helicopter contract was given, and let us know exactly what was the percentage that was given to them.

Now, I come to a very vital aspect of this entire problem. I hang my head in shame when I read in the newspapers that the Swiss Government came out with a statement that "we had unilaterally offered to the Government of India assistance in the investigation of Bofors. We do not understand why they are not accepting our offer, why they are not getting our help". They do not know that help is not necessarily welcome, some of it can be embarrassing. They are, however, feeling that way and therefore, a statement comes from the Swiss Government that "We had unilaterally offered to the Government of India that we are prepared to assist you in the investigation of these details." I do not know why you are not prepared to accept help. As far as all other spheres are concerned, we have liberalized our imports. As far as this technical assistance for moral purposes is concerned, we are not opposed to the liberalization of import of all the information from Switzerland. Full information should be sought regarding bank accounts and the issues clinched.

Recently, one event has taken place and with that I will close my observations. Here, we may indulge in hair splitting and some may try to run away with some technicalities and have cover-up operations to cover up frauds. You can indulge in such technicalities on the floor of the House, but as far as people are concerned, they are always straight-forward. Recently 18 by-elections took place in the country. Shri Vishwanath Pratap Singh has been campaigning on the issue of Bofors. During these by-elections, I campaigned among with him and the only issue that become the major issue in the elections, specially at Allahabad, was the question of corruption in high places. We said that the Prime Minister himself should squarely take responsibility for the fraud in the Bofors issue and all the malpractices that have taken place. We said in the public meetings that whosoever may be the candidate of the Congress Party, the fight in the Allahabad constituency was the fight between Shri Vishwanath Pratap Singh and the Prime Minister of the country who is responsible for all this. And it was a referendum; the Allahabad election was a referendum on Bofors, a referendum on corruption. The referendum is clear. People's opinion and the verdict is clear. Now all that this Government should do after this referendum is let them quit, face the electorate, hold a mid-term poll and then vindicate their position.

Bofors Pay-Off-IV*

At the very outset, let me point this out to you, without casting any aspersions on anyone, that as early as on 20th April 1987, at our insistence, the Defence Minister, Shri K.C. Pant, had made a written statement in this House regarding the Bofors deal, and regarding the allegations from the Swedish Radio that middlemen were involved and commission was paid. On the 17th April 1987, the Government had issued a statement, and in this very House, Shri K.C. Pant, the Defence Minister, gave a written statement in which he considered all the allegations as false and mischievous. He denied the existence of middlemen and the payment of commission.

In the afternoon, on some clarifications sought by some members, the Prime Minister also intervened and by way of clarification, he made it clear what exactly his contention was. He had recalled the talk that he had with the Prime Minister of Sweden. Then he tried to clarify that all these allegations that had been made were false. So on one occasion, he said, "You produce the evidence and we will try to examine it and try to come to the House with the truth." This is the background.

When we found that the Defence Minister and the Prime Minister made categorical statements in this House, we produced certain documents. The former Defence Minister and the former Finance

---

*Speech delivered by Prof. Madhu Dandavate in the Lok Sabha on November 15, 1988.

Minister, Vishwanath Pratap Singh, came forward with certain documents; he released them from Patna and Lucknow. He gave the account no. 999921 TU. Not only that, he came out with details; not only did he come out with the account number of the Swiss Bank Corporation and the total amount of the order of 32 million Swedish Kroners (it is coming to near about Rs. 8 crores), but he also gave a certain break-up. He gave the invoice no. 1014836 dated 8.12.86 for Kroners 47,29,190; the second invoice no. is 1010488 dated 20.3.87 for Kroners 3,53,380; the third invoice no is 1010496 dated 23.3.87 for Kroners 2,71,95,139; the total comes to about 3.2 crores of Kroners or near about Rs. 8 crores. He made it clear that he would be producing the documents and the documents are also available. Let me tell you that I have at my disposal not only what has appeared in the Press but also the original copies of the photostat copies of all these documents which the President of the Janata Dal has already produced at Lucknow and also at Patna.

I wish to make it very clear that after these documents were produced, their authenticity has not been challenged. In the past, whenever any document was produced by the members of the Opposition, there was a prompt intervention by some of the members and the professional hecklers that this was the handiwork and the fabrication of the CIA.

I was trying to point out to the House that whatever was stated by the Prime Minister and Defence Minister, Shri K.C. Pant, on 20th April 1987, was really the reiteration of their earlier statement on April 17 denying totally the existence of the middlemen and the payment of commission in the Bofors deal. I produced the documents that have been released by Shri V.P. Singh and since the question of authentication came, I once again tried to brush up my knowledge of the rules and the Hon. Speaker's Directions. Again, I got confirmed that in the course of one's speech in the House, if one quotes any relevant documents, one can always insist that those documents might be allowed to be laid on the Table of the House. Therefore, I have with me the documents regarding Svenska, A.E. Services and Lotus, all quite famous. On the basis of these, it can be clearly established that middlemen were there and in the document the word "Commission" was used. So commission was paid and the amount and dated agreement, receipts, everything, is there. Thereforee, since I have been quoting these documents, which have been used by Shri V.P. Singh and he has been asked to authenticate, I also authenticate these documents and seek your permission to lay them on the Table of the House. The usual procedure is, Mr. Speaker, you may carefully go through the documents afterwards and then you give the permission to lay them on the Table of the House and if you are convinced that this can be done, then they will be deemed as laid on the Table of the House. I follow this procedure.

Incidentally, I may remind you what your predecessors have said regarding the weight that is added by the documents that are laid on the Table of the House. The Prime Minister is not here. But I would like to make a reference to his father, a great Parliamentarian, who had followed certain Parliamentary procedures in the Parliament. When he tried to expose the famous Mundhra scandal, at the initial stage, he actually produced the circumstantial evidence and the corroborative evidence and only at the final stage was he able to produce the correspondence between the Finance Secretary and the Finance Minister. There were vocal members from the Treasury Benches, and some of the veterans objected and said, "These are confidential documents. How can Mr. Feroze Gandhi produce them and lay them on the Table of the House?" Some of them said, "Let us know what are the sources of the documents." Shri Feroze Gandhi then said to the over-enthusiastic members of the Treasury Benches, "I am not a fool to reveal my source. In that case, it will not be possible for me to expose corruption in this country." But he gave in writing to the Speaker saying, "I take full responsibility for the authenticity of the documents which I am seeking to lay on the Table of the House." Those documents were allowed to be laid on the Table. On the basis of that, the then Prime Minister said, "Accepting the authenticity of the document and the corroborative and other evidence that have been produced by Shri Feroze Gandhi, I will advise my colleague Shri T.T. Krishnamachari to resign from the Cabinet." That is what Pandit Jawaharlal Nehru had done.

I was trying to point out to you that the Prime Minister himself is my witness against the Prime Minister because what he has stated clearly runs counter to what he has been saying! Here, I may like to draw the attention of the House that the Prime Minister has consistently shifted from position to position on the Bofors issue. Initially, he said, "There are no middlemen." When it was proved that middlemen were there, he said, "no commission". When it was proved that payments were made, he mentioned, "winding up charges". When winding up charges were disproved, and it was proved that commission was paid, he said, "It must not be between Indians." When it was proved that it was paid to Indians, he said, "they are not politicians." When everything was said and done, he scored on both sides and ultimately he said that commission is paid for genuine work and industrial espionage is also considered to be a part and parcel of some genuine work. It was accepted. He seemed to be agreeing from both sides!

In our House we have one Shri Kaushal. Looking at him, I am reminded of the anecdote of a judge. To one counsel he said, "You are right. I fully agree with you. There is some substance in what you say." And when the counsel on the other side started speaking, he said, "You are right. There is substance in what you say. You seem to be right." And when someone asked, how could both of them be right, he said, "what you say is also right." That is what he said. That seems to be the position of the Prime Minister today. The way he had been shifting from position to position, ultimately coming to the conclusion that the commission was paid for genuine work, he has been contradicting what he said on the floor of the House on 20th April 1987.

In this connection, I would also like to tell you very clearly that the Prime Minister's admission, and authenticity of the document, which has not been challenged after so many days, shows that the Prime Minister and the Defence Minister have deliberately misguided the House. I do not think they have done it innocently. The have deliberately made wrong and untruthful statements in the House.

There is no path left open to the Prime Minister and the Defense Minister on this issue because of the breach of privilege.

As far as investigations are concerned, the Swedish authorities have gone on record that they were prepared to help investigation processes, but we have not taken advantage of that. Again the Swiss Government has categorically said that they are prepared to give necessary assistance to find out the facts in respect of payment of commission in the Bofors deal. I do not know why we did not take advantage of that. We know that in the Philippines a big fraud was perpetrated by the ruler there. We find that Marcos's entire wealth that was hidden as black money in international financial institutions was actually dug out and the facts came to light not only before the Filipinos but also before the entire world. In this case, V.P. Singh's behaviour throughout has been exemplary.

Even when V.P. Singh was sitting on the Treasury Benches, he acted on the dictates of his conscience. And when the time came, he spoke out his mind. He threw away the Defence Ministership and he tried to tell the truth to the people. In this history, V.P. Singh's name will go on record as a clean man who had given vent to the dictates of his conscience to maintain his image in public life.

I shall conclude by saying that the manner in which Vishwanath Pratap Singh conducted himself when the Bofors episode took place, when he was on the Treasury Benches and when he quit the Treasury Benches and joined the Opposition, his behaviour has been exemplary, moral and ethical. And so long as these standards are maintained in the country, men like V.P. Singh will be able to mobilise public opinion in the country. Once it is mobilised, there will be no other alternative for the Prime Minister but to quit his post, go and seek the mandate of the people and get rejected by the people. That will be the fate that the Prime Minister will have to meet. I am sure this will happen.

INDEX